TOGETHER IN THE DARK

Together in the Dark

MYSTERIES OF HEALING

Robert H. Colfelt, M.D.

MADRONA PUBLISHERS • SEATTLE

Published by
Madrona Publishers, Inc.
P.O. Box 22667
Seattle, Washington 98122

10 9 8 7 6 5 4 3 2 1

Library of Congress Cataloging-in-Publication Data

Colfelt, Robert H.
Together in the dark.

1. Colfelt, Robert H.   2. Physicians — United States —
Biography.   3. Medicine — United States.   4. Healing —
United States.   I. Title.
R154.C5413A3   1987   610'.1   87-5801
ISBN 0-88089-021-5

For Mary and our children
Kurt, Brenda, Colleen and Todd

Contents

In a dark time, the eye begins to see . . .

THEODORE ROETHKE, "In a Dark Time"

PART ONE

I'm Not Beethoven

Mrs. Bachman

THE spring sun warms the ground as best it can. It is a time of beginnings. The Troy-Bilt tiller starts on the first pull and attacks the soil with determination. I just walk along beside it, adjust the throttle and watch this machine work. It won't stop on its own and knows nothing of the direction it goes. It will go off of a cliff or into a river if given a chance. And it could destroy a golf course as well as till a garden. The steel blades pulverize the grass clumps until the earth is a part of Eden, unspoiled and unused.

Several types of chickens watch from their muddy pen. Give them grain, grit, mash, and a little water and they will construct the best eggs you've ever eaten. Let's see a bureaucrat do that. Left to her own devices, a hen will emerge one day from her hiding place under the barn and lead a new brood of chicks into the daylight.

Gnarled fruit trees in the sloping orchard grow in disarray. No time to prune them again this year. But we will have fresh apples from August until winter freezes the remaining hanger-oners to the ground. All we need are bees and no frost after the fruit is set.

Some thirty feet off the ground, in the eaves of our red farmhouse, swallows and wrens build their nests, while noisy robins use the tree branches. A time for birds. The widgeons who spent winter days feeding in our flooded pasture have headed back north and frogs have moved in. The water has subsided and the frogs croak all night. A time for frogs. Horses relish the fresh grass, a welcome change from dry alfalfa.

As I walk along behind my tiller, the practice of neurology is far away. The clouds seem as lazy as I am. Sometimes farming is more fun thinking about than doing. Suddenly I think of Mrs. Bachman. Why, after all these years, I don't know, but there she is in my mind.

When a patient such as Mrs. Bachman swirls in, lands comfortably in the chair across from my desk, hands me a large package of medical records, crosses her legs, lights a cigarette and begins, "It all started in the spring of 1946 and I can't go on any longer..." my enthusiasm flags.

She was the first office patient of the day. A bulging middle-aged doctor-goer, whose list of symptoms seemed to grow with each breath. Her search for the "cure" to her mysterious ailment had led her through most local clinics and medical centers. Because of the physician's usual fascination for numbers, just about everything one could think of about Mrs. Bachman had been measured, counted, weighed, analyzed, calculated, X rayed and recorded. But to no avail. The answer still eluded the best medical minds. Her struggle against her undiagnosed illness drove her ever onward. She paid little attention to me as she charged ahead, digressing, regressing, elaborating, giving the opinion of this specialist or that professor and mentioning diseases I'd never heard of.

Meanwhile, I was having my own problems. It was my first day in the office wearing my new contact lenses, the hard kind. Her cigarette smoke found its way to my eyes, and I fought hard to keep back my tears. I wiped my nose once or twice.

After a while she heard me sniff. She asked if I was all right. I assured her I was and invited her to go on with her medical history. As she began to recount a particularly involved description of her great pain from "progressive arthritis of the spinal cord," I looked up to reach for a kleenex. My cheeks glistened with tears. I smiled, wiped them dry and batted my eyes a few times to adjust the slippery lenses.

"You dear thing!" she exclaimed, her face sober and her eyes moist. She took a supply of kleenex for herself, dabbed a bit here and there and said, "I want you to know that you are the kindest, most sympathetic man I have ever met. Gawd! If only we had more doctors like you!"

"I get it from my mother," I replied. We blew our noses in concert.

She leaned across my desk, put her hand on my wrist and patted me gently. "Most doctors aren't even interested in my case. They just read the reports, nod a few times and say they can't do anything. Or else they put me through a lot of expensive and painful tests and try me on some medicine I'm allergic to ... don't let me forget to tell you about my allergies."

"I probably can't do anything either," I volunteered.

"Don't you feel bad about that," she said. "Just try the best you can and I'll understand." She gave me a grandmotherly smile and I half expected to get a kiss on the forehead or a glass of milk and a cookie.

After I finished examining her, she asked for my diagnosis. I didn't have one. Had I ever seen a case like hers before? No, I couldn't say I had. Did she need to come back and see me? I couldn't think why.

As we parted, she turned and said, "Tell me doctor, do you think I will have to learn to live with this, whatever it is?"

"You already have," I said, red-eyed and stuffy-nosed.

"That's right, I have, haven't I? I've been through all they could do to me, but I'm still here." She laughed.

"It takes a healthy person to go through all that and still be on their feet," I replied.

"It does, doesn't it?" she said as she swept down the hall.

Wherever you are, Mrs. Bachman, I wish you well.

Who Is the President?

THE chronic-care ward of a hospital. An old woman, disheveled and impatient, searches her breakfast tray for the cup of lukewarm coffee. She is strapped into the chair next to her bed. Her movements are stiff and clumsy, her vision poor, and she shakes with the tremor of Parkinson's disease.

The oatmeal is cold, lumpy and flooded with skim milk. The overcooked egg, still in its shell, lies split down the middle in a pile of yolk crumbs. The toast is smeared with margarine. A bowl of mandarin oranges crouches to her left where she cannot see it. Her drugged mind fights to help her feed herself.

After she eats what she can, she is whisked off by wheelchair to the shower where she sits on a stool and is scrubbed, dried and dressed in a clean white gown slit up the back. Her feet are placed in paper slippers and she is wheeled back to her room.

The physical therapist arrives, takes her by the arm and attempts to soothe her with kind words she cannot hear because the battery in her hearing aid is dead. She smiles a pleasant toothless response and holds onto the strong arm supporting her while she tries to cover her exposed buttocks by reaching behind to close the gaping gown.

Back in her chair, she is greeted by the nurse who brings morning medicines. She swallows them with a gulp and complains about her breakfast. The nurse replies that her diet is professionally planned to avoid vitamin deficiency, protein imbalance and excessive cholesterol. To eat only what she wants leads to malnutrition.

The doctor visits her on rounds, careful not to touch her. He is formal, excessively jovial, and talks more to the nurse than to her. Even in her twilight awareness she anticipates his test of her mental condition: "Who is the president?" Her sluggish memory ponders how there ever came to be such an assemblage of doctors, nurses and others who don't know who is the president, and once told, promptly forget.

He leans forward and shouts the question in her ear. She forces a smile, and he repeats it louder and more slowly. She studies the two blurs in front of her and replies, "Harry Roosevelt." The doctor and nurse glance knowingly at each other, pat her on the shoulder.

The nurse asks her to name the day of the week. The woman looks down at her hands, wondering what difference the day makes in a place where all days are the same for her. She is not permitted to walk in her garden, gather flowers or wander through small shops admiring what she can never afford. Even the months no longer matter. October and March are indistinguishable these days. She shrugs her shoulders. The doctor writes new orders in her chart and leaves.

After lunch she is trapped by the piercing babble of television because her hearing-aid battery has been replaced and the volume turned all the way up. Her trembling fingers cannot find the control.

The evening nurse roughly puts her to bed, irritated that the woman would not urinate when taken to the bathroom. The nurse is strong in body and by virtue of her authority. She can make people do many things, but she cannot make the old woman urinate.

The woman is poseyed into the neatly sheeted bed, surrounded with padded rails, her head elevated to prevent pulmonary congestion. The invading night blackens all but the night light. She drifts off into pleasant memories of when Harry Roosevelt was president and how he would never permit people to be treated like this. But Harry Roosevelt is gone and so is everyone else who might help her. She is on her own and there is no escape, only resistance. She empties her full bladder into the bed and falls asleep.

Intensive Care

EARLY afternoon. The summer wind flies down on the bay on the wings of the incoming tide. Water that was serene and calm an hour ago bristles into whitecaps while evergreen trees along the shore wave them home. The beach disappears under the murk of sea that lifts up the dried sand and sets it down where it will. The beach is never the same after each tide.

I've finished my oyster stew, made fresh from the passive beach residents I collected during the minus-2.7-foot tide. My arguments about the dangers of cholesterol were easily dispensed with as the aroma of cooking oysters filled the kitchen. Now that my stomach is full I resolve to watch my diet more carefully. The comfortable seldom make effective zealots.

There were no protests from the oysters when I shucked them. Their becoming my lunch seemed well within the possibilities of their fate. I don't think oysters should complain about things like that.

The phrase "intensive care" settles in my mind. I woke up thinking about it and it will not leave. Even here on the deck, where I bask in the breeze while avoiding all routine obligations, the words "intensive care" drum in my head.

The only one I have to talk to at the moment is my dog, mostly German shepherd, with a bit of coyote, and she isn't interested. She lies near the edge of the deck where she can watch the road in front of this cabin. Whenever a jogger or bicycler goes by, she lifts her head, barks and lowers her long snout between her outstretched paws while she waits for the next one. What all of this has to do with the tide coming in and the oysters digesting in my innards is not clear. But sometimes thoughts take hold of me, and when they do, I find it best to listen until their meaning becomes clear.

Then she appears. Not here of course, but in my memory, an elderly lady who suffers seizures because of a scar in her brain from a small stroke. Her care would be uneventful if she would take her anticonvulsants as prescribed. But for reasons known only to herself, she periodically decides the medicine is not helping her and stops taking it. Within a few days she has a convulsion at home, her husband calls 911 and soon she is in the hospital Emergency Room.

One day she arrived in the ER after having a seizure at home and promptly suffered a second. The house officer mistakenly made a diagnosis of status epilepticus (seizures coming one after the other so rapidly the patient's brain suffers from lack of oxygen and serious brain swelling may result) and administered a large dose of intravenous anticonvulsants. Of course this prevented further seizures, a desirable result, but it also induced hypotension and marked lethargy, potentially serious complications.

When I arrived at the hospital she was in the Intensive Care Unit, unarousable, with the appropriate monitoring devices in place. Gradually she began to thrash around in the bed, and soon her nasal oxygen was rerouted to her right ear, which I thought ought to have looked pinker than the other one but didn't.

I tried to settle her down by yelling directly into her ear words of encouragement and understanding; she was also nearly deaf. But she either didn't understand me or else just ignored what I said.

The nurse and I were trying to gain control of the situation, but the patient was as drunk on anticonvulsants as she might have been on gin. Just when we thought we could relax our vigil, she would try to raise up, twisting and thrashing against the restraints. We worried about her heart giving out as well as about her injuring herself during these violent paroxysms.

I looked up during one of these unequal wrestling matches and saw her husband standing next to the bed, watching in horror. Tears ran down his cheeks. He was well into his eighties, a rim of white hair above his ears, lean, with the big hands of a Scandinavian fisherman. He wore thick glasses and hearing aids in both ears, and his nose ran as uncontrolled as his tears.

He watched as the nurse and I debated what to do. More sedation might make matters worse, yet our efforts to contain her squirming were at best a draw, with the end nowhere in sight. He pushed past me and clutched her hand with one of his while he swept the moisture from his face with a large handkerchief held in the other. Then he called her name.

She roused, eyes barely open, and with a huge toothless grin turned toward the familiar voice. He bent over the bed and they kissed, oxygen, restraints and monitors be damned. She sighed and settled peacefully back into bed while they continued to squeeze each others' hands. Soon she drifted into a pleasant sleep with traces of the smile still across her face.

We had no more problems with her agitation and the following morning we moved her to the neurology ward. Over the next few days she became her old self, and her husband beamed at her progress. He sat for long hours at her side, and often they said little to each other.

They were not interested in the social-service workers helping them with their "living situation." Her husband promised me he would make sure she took the medicine, although she remained unpersuaded about its necessity. If it was so important, she asked, why didn't she have seizures more often?

The morning she was discharged I asked her if she remembered her husband kissing her in the Intensive Care Unit. No, she didn't, but it was just like the old fool to embarrass the two of them that way. She laughed.

I recall the opening lines of a Richard Hugo poem:

> You come here Sunday on a whim.
> Say your life broke down. The last good kiss
> you had was years ago.

Continuing Medical Education

ALTHOUGH she liked me and respected my medical abilities, she was dissatisfied with my assessment and management of her case. An intelligent, ring-wise middle-aged counsellor, she had not been relieved of her cervical and shoulder pain by a two-level fusion performed on her osteoarthritic neck four months earlier. Subsequently she came to see me about her chronic pain. She had been unable to return to work, took large amounts of pain medicine and could not find comfort in bed with or without the cervical collar she was addicted to during the day. She was seriously depressed.

One other complicating factor was that the clinical indications for her surgery were marginal in the first place and like many patients who do not improve following surgery, she was resentful and bitter. But it was too late to reconsider. Her hope for a corrective operation was pure fantasy and she knew it.

I admitted her to a hospital, ordered further X rays to compare with the previous ones, arranged for physical therapy, placed her in cervical traction, ordered a consultation or two and applied some of my most ingenious combinations of medicines. She and I spent considerable time discussing the effects of pain upon depression and depression upon pain. After a complicated ten or twelve days in this intensive program she was discharged somewhat improved — or so we thought.

Two weeks later, she sat next to her husband in my office, her legs crossed, tearfully smoking a cigarette, and told me that she could no longer pretend she was getting better because she wasn't. Instead, she had more pain in her neck, extending across her back and down into her arms. Her only relief was to stupify herself with drugs. She regarded her persistent symptoms as a personal failure. She could not accomplish the psychological adjustments within herself that she frequently asked her clients to make.

Her husband, a bright and sensible man, was wary and disappointed when, after I finished re-examining his wife, I reiterated that although her pain was real — patients know how and what they feel — its driving mechanism was her unresolved anger and frustration. All the evidence indicated that was the case and I was long experienced in treating patients with chronic musculoskeletal pain. I was tough about her use of addicting medicines and placed the responsibility for her improvement, or lack of it, squarely upon her shoulders. Perhaps another physician could do better by her. In any event, a visit to a psychiatrist was in order if she was serious about all of this.

She countered that she had no objection to visiting a psychiatrist, she was in a similar business herself, but no one could talk her out of the pain. It was there and unrelentingly so. Finally she came to her point. She said that she knew something else was wrong. She didn't know how she knew but she knew. Despite the trickeries of her mind such pain as this could not be just a function of emotional distress.

Her husband confirmed that after she arrived home from

the hospital, she was optimistic and tried to do more things. However, as the reality that her pain was not improving set in, her depression remobilized and drove her down. She had seen tough times in her life before and knew what it was to suffer, overcome and profit from struggles. She was no office-neurotic and was not depressive by nature. In fact, her considerable effectiveness as a counsellor was in no small part due to her ability to empathize with and encourage her clients. She was a woman one could believe in and trust. And, he added, her brain might be far more likely to fool me than the two of them.

By now, I was well behind in my schedule and my secretary slipped me a note indicating several patients in the waiting room were alternating irritated glances between their watches and each other. I agreed to readmit this suffering woman to the hospital and we parted after formulating a plan none of us much believed in.

Two days later shock overwhelmed my embarrassment as I read the radioactive bone-scan report: multiple meta-static lesions throughout the skeletal system, most marked in the cervical spine. Later an oncologist would locate with difficulty a small primary tumor in one of her breasts.

I presented the report to the patient and her husband. They were right and I was wrong. So were all the other doctors who had examined her. I had discovered what she already knew. It was especially heart-breaking for her husband because his first wife had died a number of years earlier from carcinoma of the breast. At last, the enemy was apparent and it was a far different one than I had thought.

Over the next few days we talked about what the future might hold: chemotherapy, surgery, irradiation, continued deterioration of her spine with nerve-root or spinal-cord compression, even quadriplegia and death. Throughout the next many weeks she experienced the indignities, disappointments and agony of undergoing extensive treatment with no certainty of success. She lost all her hair from chemotherapy, suffered a terribly sore tongue and loss of taste from irradiation, and spent weeks in bed with a metal halo screwed into her head and supported by four metal rods attached to a body cast to prevent her cervical spine from collapse.

If there was any healing energy in resolve, she discovered it. Her husband's patience and encouragement were enormously helpful.

Finally, she went into remission and, I suspect, became a better counsellor than ever.

A Christmas Present

LATE one December evening several years ago I walked aboard the ferryboat *Walla Walla* at Pier 52 in Seattle, on my way home at last. The day had begun with hospital rounds, followed by a full schedule in the office, many telephone calls, evening rounds, and concluded with a board meeting of some sort — complete with cocktails, prime rib and wine. I had the heavy feet and slow mind that come from such days. Now I sat alone in the nearly empty boat. After removing my heavy coat, I loosened my tie, slipped off my shoes and settled back on a bench near a window.

Rain obscured the bright orange lights illuminating the piers where container ships were unloaded. The inside of the window was heavy with condensation. My reflection was dim and I looked more tired than I realized. My choice was reading the newspaper or taking a nap during the thirty-minute crossing. Despite the inconvenience of traveling to and from work by ferryboat, I enjoyed the sense of leaving one world and entering another whenever the boat eased from the dock. Soon I would be home by the fire.

Her voice had an easily recognizable lilt highlighting her precise diction. As I looked up, she removed her coat and sat down opposite me, continuing her friendly greeting, asking if

I thought it would snow. I said I did because I always hoped it would snow. She was about sixty, charming and intelligent. I knew she had lived a difficult life. Widowed early, she gradually became self-sufficient in the business world and raised her son without a father. We occasionally saw each other at discussion groups and informal social events. She was intractably cheerful, a quality I'd never been able to master myself and thus found difficult to bear in others. My usual reaction to such a bundle of upbeat enthusiasm was to first feel ill at ease, soon irritated and in the end, depressed. Despite the fact I liked her and always found her interesting, tonight I wanted her to leave me alone. But she mistook my indolence for receptivity and began a narrative I soon knew I was to hear in its entirety. I decided not to be rude, and so now and then I raised an eyebrow or muttered an exclamation. She smiled broadly as she talked on in sentences, paragraphs and even pages. Her story was about her son and her sister. Although what follows is only a summary of her narrative, as it is beyond my scope to give a full account, most of the details are correct. I think you will see why I became drawn into her story.

First of all, her son. He was a bright young man who became a minister in one of the standard Protestant denominations and enjoyed excellent success in his first parish in a small town in the East. However, according to his mother, he lacked some of the more spiritual aspects of his faith, favoring social-action programs and community organizations. He loved the Rotary and the Chamber of Commerce. Indeed, he was a son to be proud of, especially when one considered the obstacles he overcame to acquire his education. He was, in fact, a success.

Now his aunt, the storyteller's sister, was a different

matter altogether. She led what the mental health experts would describe as the life of "an impulse-ridden character disorder." In short, she was a hell-raiser with lots of lovers, lots of booze and lots of good times. (Momentarily I envied her.) However, she suffered much sadness from broken marriages and her self-destructive habits. As her health generally and her liver specifically declined over the years she prematurely aged and her beauty all but disappeared. Physicians, tired of her ignoring their instructions, soon paid little heed to her. As she became more ill she consulted a physician who didn't know her. He determined she was terminally ill from metastatic cancer. Whether earlier diagnosis would have improved her chances, I didn't find out.

The young minister had long been fond of his aunt. Maybe he envied her, too. Be that as it may, when he learned of her desperate condition, he promptly flew to Southern California where she was hospitalized. The fate of her soul was at stake. He tried the usual aphorisms and familiar reassurances; however the words sounded hollow and bloodless. To her he was a nephew, not a man of God. She seemed to have few regrets except toward those people she'd treated poorly, but the details of their conversations remained a secret.

As death approached she slept long periods and he sat by her bed. Periodically she would rouse and they would talk. Days passed and another presence emerged in the room. At first he wasn't sure what was happening and thought his feeling was simply an emotional reaction. As he listened to the stricken woman's labored breathing and stared out the window at the streets filled with people scurrying onward in their lives, he realized the presence emerging from this cancer-ridden woman was a mystical spirit he had never encountered before. Despite her grave condition, when she did rouse, she became more consoling to him than he to her. What they shared is forever unknown, perhaps even indescribable. He was too frightened to tell anyone else about it.

She was lucid for a time on her last day. She explained to him how in preceding days she felt herself detach from her body only to return because she had more to tell him. He would no longer speak with her, only sit, hold her hand and listen. After she finished dying, he sat by her side and was enveloped by the spirit more powerfully present than ever. This special joy left him wordless. After a time the presence left and his life changed.

The *Walla Walla* rounded the entrance buoy and reduced speed as it entered Eagle Harbor. She stood and slipped on her coat as she prepared to descend to the car deck. My car was in a parking lot in Winslow and I would walk off the boat. I thanked her for telling me about her son and his aunt. I suggested that her own minister would be interested in hearing what she'd told me. As she pulled on her wool cap and gathered her purse, she replied that she would never tell him because he didn't believe in such things. But she thought I had the kind of mind that considered many things and would take her seriously. I assured her that I did. Then she said that she might be a little dingy, but one has to be if one wants to see and feel what is important in life. She bustled off.

As I walked from the terminal up the steep parking lot toward my car, I noticed that the rain had been transformed into snow and a pale blanket illuminated everything exposed to weather. There was no wind. I looked back at the *Walla Walla* moored tight against the dock, which though brightly lit was barely visible in the falling snow.

The words of Father Brown, G. K. Chesterton's diminutive detective, seemed a part of that night: "I always believe in the impossible but not the improbable."

Quick Response Time

THE assortment of liquids drips down my nasogastric tube into my stomach. My blood vessels are punched regularly to obtain laboratory specimens and infuse medicines. The urinary catheter is no bargain, and it is embarrassing to watch myself empty my bowels in the bed. My cardiac monitor beeps constantly and my efficient respirator won't let me finish dying. Maybe I'm vain, but I resent those who care for me leaving my blankets messed up when they are finished. After all, I can't cover myself.

The doctors and nurses often make nervous jokes at my bedside. They know I am in a coma. Imagine how surprised they would be if they knew I was perched on the oxygen jet watching them.

You must understand how it is for me. I've been trying to leave ever since I arrived in the Intensive Care Unit. Those in charge consider my death to be when my heart stops. But every time it does, they jolt me with electricity and inject drugs that start it up again. It is my hard luck that my heart responds so effectively. As long as my heart beats I am kept tethered to this mindless wreck of a body.

Let me back up a bit. I was the victim of "quick response time." One night three weeks ago I woke up feeling as though there was a horse standing on my chest. I breathed in brief gasps and was desperately weak. My wife called the medics, but before they arrived I drifted into a coma still clutching her hand. My mind and spirit were on their way.

The medics knew their stuff, and within minutes I was zapped, intubated, injected and on my way in the ambulance with swirling lights and blaring sirens. That part was exciting.

In the Emergency Room I was surrounded by more doctors and nurses than I could count. They were magnificent in their skills and dedication to saving my life. But they neglected to determine that my brain was no longer working, and without my brain, the rest of my body is not worth much. I could forgive that, seeing their youth and inexperience, and it was fine with me to go along with their efforts for a time. Never did I dream it would lead to this.

My attending physician is an excellent man. His credentials are the best, and everyone here respects him. He has gray hair, earned the hard way, I expect. The house staff crowds around him on rounds, and he tells them about my heart and its disease. He discusses the treatment of potential complications in my case. I found that interesting until I realized one morning that he had no intention of letting me finish dying. For him, life equals heartbeats.

Several consultants examined me, and in some way I haven't figured out, each one took responsibility for that part of me each regarded as his specialty. According to the lung doctor my breathing is better. The kidney doctor says my urine output and electrolyte balance are fine. The infectious-disease doctor has me on the proper antibiotics. Each morning my wife receives reports that I am improving in these specific ways. But my coma persists.

My wife is too smart for them. She knows the truth, and when she asks about my eventual recovery, each doctor says only time will tell. This morning she shook them a bit when she said time has already had its chance. I wanted to take her in my arms, which of course is impossible.

My doctor sometimes stands at my bedside, and when others are not around he appears near tears. But he also seems powerless to stop the machines which have taken charge of us all. He tries to hide the strain from others, which I'm not sure is a good idea. He should conserve his energies for those who can be saved and let me go. I know he will be relieved when I finally die and he no longer has to confront my wretchedness every day.

Now I understand the night my father died. After I received the phone call, I fell asleep sobbing. He came into my dreams, young and happy, celebrating his freedom from his senile brain, stumbling gait, failing vision and hearing, and hospital restraints. "I'm free and I'm fine," he shouted to me, looking young and healthy. During his funeral and at visits to his grave I wept for my loss, and much of my grief was selfish even though I pretended it wasn't.

It fills me with sadness to watch my family grieve at my bedside. But their grief cannot proceed until my body gives out.

The Woman Who Knew What She Wanted

AT first glance she looked like a Hungarian duchess from the last century, not so much in the way she dressed as in her slow elegant walk and regal smile. It was clear she was European, old European. Her age? Sixty-five at least. She gave the impression of one who changed little from decade to decade, and then only in the character of the lines around her eyes and mouth and the graying of her hair. Even her bosom, waist and hips were classical in configuration, and if her figure depended upon a series of pressures and paddings, it was not apparent.

She introduced herself formally as she stood facing the middle-aged physician, his cluttered desk a barrier between them. She settled into a sagging chair, opened her purse and lifted out an envelope of medical reports which she passed to him with a slight nod.

He accepted the reports with a similar nod. While he thumbed through them, glancing at this page and that, she sat erect, her white gloved hands folded across her lap, and studied a painting of swimming mallards that hung on the wall to the left of his desk.

The physician was a self-satisfied man who enjoyed seeing patients whom other physicians had not handled as well as they might. He skillfully pointed out others' lack of judgement, even ineptitude, when he detected it, and he orchestrated new regimens of diagnostic and therapeutic attacks, usually to the delight of the patients and their families. They felt blessed that they had come to his attention, and he radiated agreement as he handed them his bill.

According to her medical records, one night at home her right arm had suddenly begun to jerk uncontrollably. Her husband called 911, and the Aid Car took her to a local hospital emergency room. The doctor on duty diagnosed a partial epileptic seizure and treated her with intravenous medicine. After the seizure stopped she wanted to go home, but her husband insisted she heed the doctor's advice and be admitted as a patient. She reluctantly agreed.

Dye was injected into the arteries that supplied her brain and X rays taken. During this procedure, she suffered another jerking attack involving both the right arm and leg, leaving her with a modest paralysis of her right side and some difficulty in speaking. She knew what she wanted to say, but could not form the words. She thought she had had a stroke.

These deficits took all day to clear. After her ability to speak returned, she insisted on a conference with her doctor. She accused him of causing her stroke. He said she hadn't suffered a stroke. She asked him who was in a better position to judge than the person it happened to. She was upset about her husband leaving on a long business trip: she would be left alone, and his health was not good, either. Was that not enough to cause the seizure? The doctor said no.

The doctor wanted her to come back to his office in a month, but she came back in a week, telling him she worried about another stroke or seizure. Again she insisted the doctor instruct her husband not to go on the trip. He refused, maintaining the trip was incidental, and the real problem was that she wanted to tell everyone what to do.

Despite her better judgement, she returned for a third office visit because her husband insisted that she was in good hands. To her dismay she found that her blood pressure was still elevated above normal, and the doctor insisted on increasing the dosage of a medicine which she was convinced made her dizzy. When she returned home, she discussed all of this with her husband and he promised to find her another doctor. He called the medical society referral service that suggested this clinic.

Her position now was simple. She and her husband wanted a doctor who would explain things to her and discuss what should be done. She pointed out that both she and her husband were fluent in English. They had learned it in Europe before the war, and they were both capable of intelligent discussion.

The physician made notes while she talked, underlining here and there in her medical records. Next he examined her thoroughly and said that he would try to help her. She was to collect her X-ray studies from the hospital and bring them to him in two days. He would then discuss her entire case in as much detail as necessary and offer his plan for treatment. He suggested that her husband should come with her. She was immensely pleased.

Two days later, she and her husband, a lean man with a thin face and discolored teeth, sat side by side awaiting the physician's analysis. They both smiled as he covered each point to their satisfaction. It was as she had thought: the other doctor did not care enough to properly inform her. In her opinion another medicine for her high blood pressure was indicated, one that would not make her dizzy. And she made one more point. She knew her cholesterol level was too high and she wanted medicine to bring it down to normal. With that, the nurse took her next door for a blood test and blood-pressure reading. Her husband sat where he was.

"She thinks you should stay home instead of making your business trip," said the physician.

"I know. She is a woman of strong opinions, as you can see. But I will do so if you think it advisable." His accent was thick Slavic.

"Good. Now, the man who cared for her in the hospital is a fine doctor."

"True enough, but not right for her," answered her husband.

"Why do you say that?"

"She wants a doctor whom she can trust. For her, the one to be trusted is the one who hides nothing from her."

"But I won't make any major changes in her care. His diagnosis and treatment are essentially correct." He lifted his left cuff and consulted his watch, a way he had devised of letting patients know the visit was nearing its end.

Her husband caught the maneuver, then unbuttoned his left cuff and rolled up his left sleeve, exposing a series of numbers tattooed on his forearm.

"Do you know what these numbers mean?"

The physician nodded.

"I was a grave digger in the camps. In the winter we built enormous fires to thaw the frozen ground. After we dug the graves, the prisoners were lined up along the edge and shot, causing them to fall backwards. We covered them even if they were not dead."

The physician rubbed his fingers across his damp brow.

"My wife had a more difficult time than I did. After

three years in the Nazi camps, she was liberated by the Russians, who sent her to the Gulag. Jews were not well liked by either side."

"I can imagine."

"Then your imagination is better than mine, doctor. She still has nightmares about doctors who abused her in ways I don't care to know about. I do know she was sterilized by the Nazis. They used her for experiments." He lit a cigarette, ignoring the "Thanks For Not Smoking" sign directly in front of him.

The physician leaned back as far as he could in his chair.

"In the Gulag she survived by having, shall we say, a close relationship with the commandant. As you can see, she is still a lovely woman."

"How long have you been married?"

"We were lovers before the war. Then we were separated for several years. I thought she was dead because I did not know about the Gulag until I met a man who had escaped. He told me she would be released as part of a trade for Nazi soldiers. I waited in her village a year, nearly starved and worked on a road crew. Always a shovel for me. After she returned, it took much time for her to overcome her shame. We decided to marry and come to America for a new life."

The physician had not taken his eyes from this man, except when he reached into his drawer for an ashtray which he placed on the desk.

The man extinguished his cigarette, held both hands up in front of him with the palms toward the physician. "That was all long ago. I've said too much and I apologize for taking your time. You are a good listener, doctor, and I see why she likes you. The other doctor was not interested in how she came to be as she is about medical matters. He wanted her to take tranquilizers."

The office door opened, and the woman peeked in.

"Are you two having a nice conversation?" There was music in her voice.

"The doctor has advised me that you are right. I should not go on the trip for both of our benefits. So, it is settled. We will do without the money and eat soup for a month." He laughed and she kissed his cheek.

"Your husband was telling me a bit about your time during the war," said the physician.

"Just give me adequate instructions, please. If I know what I am to do, I can do it." She started to cry. "I don't like to cry, doctor, but it is terrible to be at the mercy of others. Do you believe that, doctor?"

The Surgeon and the Fat Man

EACH morning the night nurse on the chronic-care ward shook her head sadly when she saw the surgeon coming. There was no change to report in his patient either for the better, which was impossible, or for the worse, which was what the staff caring for the patient hoped for.

The fat man lay withering in flaccid unawareness. It was uncanny how he seemed at times to follow whoever was in the room with his eyes. But he never gave any sign of recognition to the surgeon or nurses. His wife reported that he would smile and blow kisses to her, but no one else believed that, for they knew her to be simple and unable to accept his fate.

The surgeon was well trained and well liked by patients and colleagues alike, and for good reason. He was dedicated beyond the point of self-sacrifice. He always maintained his professional courtesy and dignity. He stayed long at the hospital with desperately ill patients and welcomed calls at home by the nursing staff. He was always ready for surgery and never hesitated to stop whatever he was doing that was unrelated to his practice and race to the hospital. As a consequence, his wife and five children had formed a family without him and long since given up resenting his absence.

They didn't much care any more if he was around or not. In fact, it was easier in some ways when he did not intrude into their lives.

The fat man was admitted on the morning of the day surgery was scheduled. The surgeon had agreed to take him ahead of the abdominal aneurysm because the fat man was so frightened. There was no comfort for this terrified man, and when the surgeon attempted to explain the possible complications the fat man looked away and said he didn't want to hear about it.

The fat man was in his fifties and he'd lived a rough life. He had forty pounds of belly from beer and strong sausage and scarred lungs from lots of cigarettes. Even after his third bout of cholecystitis, with the danger of a stone lodging in his common duct looming ever larger, it took his wife's tears, his two massive brothers' insistence, and assurance from his parish priest of God's intense interest in the matter for him to sign the consent form. The family and priest advised the surgeon to tell the fat man that everything would be fine and get on with surgery.

While the nurses prepared him for his operation, his wife, brothers and priest were at his bedside. The priest read consoling verses from the scriptures, glancing at his watch every few minutes, for he had plans of his own.

The fall salmon were entering the river and his fishing partner waited in the car with poles, hip boots and tackle ready. As soon as the fat man was whisked down the hall the priest would slip down the back stairs and the two fishermen would be on their way.

The nurse gave the fat man an injection in his buttock, after which he made her turn her back while he removed his dentures and placed them in a plastic cup. After that he would not talk except with his lips pressed tightly together. His wife said that he might only be a long-haul driver, but he had his pride. The fat man objected to the gown split down the back for it was of less than sufficient size to cover both his belly and his large hips. The priest suggested a tent but the fat man did not think that idea was funny.

When the orderly started to push the cart toward the door, the fat man kissed his wife three times, shook hands with both brothers and implored the priest to continue praying until the surgery was finished and he was safe. The priest replied that continuous prayers were not necessary because God had an excellent memory. He neglected to mention that even a priest cannot flycast and cross himself at the same time.

The surgeon suffered a terrible shock when, after he finished the aneurysm case, he found the fat man still unresponsive in the recovery room. There were no apparent biochemical or physiological imbalances to be found, and two consultants offered detailed notes brimming with speculation but devoid of answers. The anesthesia machines were checked, the drugs given verified, the postoperative monitoring discussed with the nurses and a toxic drug screen taken on the fat man's blood. There were no clues.

Even the most detailed restrospective analysis shed no light on why the fat man never woke up after surgery. There had been a brief period of cyanosis and more blood loss than expected, but neither the anesthetist nor the surgeon regarded either event as important at the time. There were a few suspicious glances between them, but no accusations were made.

The fat man was given stimulants, drugs to combat brain swelling, drugs to increase urine output, oxygen and antibiotics, all to no avail. The most reasonable explanation seemed to be a stroke deep in the activating system of the brain. That is the diagnosis usually made by neurologists when they can't think of anything else to say, and the surgeon found that opinion unenlightening.

That evening, the surgeon, anesthetist and two consultants assembled the family for a meeting. Needless to say it was a painful time for all concerned. To make matters worse, the surgeon had sent word to the fat man's wife, just after the final stitches were sewn, that he was fine and only needed to sleep off the anesthesia. The brothers had gone back to the service station they jointly owned while his wife remained at the hospital and visited on the phone with well-wishers. The priest didn't know what had happened because he was still fishing.

The brothers said they were not surprised about the outcome. They could both remember comrades in military combat who thought they might be killed on a certain day and often were. One brother said that some people know when terrible things are going to happen to them and this just proved it. The wife was stunned by the news but felt much better when she saw her husband resting comfortably in bed and in no apparent discomfort or distress. She thought he might just wake up any time because he often fell asleep in his chair at home for no reason and was always hard to wake up.

The priest didn't find out what happened until later that evening when one of the brothers called him at home where he was dressing three fine bright salmon. The priest put the salmon in the refrigerator and went to the chapel to pray. He visited the family at the hospital, gave the fat man last rites and went back home where he had trouble enjoying his salmon dinner.

The fat man was given intravenous fluids, nutritional supplements through a feeding tube and all other measures to sustain him in hopes he would awaken. After a week of no improvement the surgeon suggested to the family that the treatments be discontinued as they were not helping his severely damaged brain, and the strain was terrible for everyone. He dismissed the wife's optimism as unfounded. No one answered his comments. They all stared at the floor until one of the brothers asked to speak to the surgeon in the hall.

In hushed voices, the two brothers told how the fat man was mean and unkind to his wife. He drank a lot, knocked her around and criticized her endlessly because she was dull-witted and slow. She endured the marriage because divorce was against the Church, and the priest tried to counsel her without success. The priest said that enduring hardship with God's help was part of life and things could always be worse. Somehow she kept her cheerfulness, and even now still believed that her husband would wake up soon.

The older of the two brothers said he had gone through the fat man's personal papers trying to sort out business matters and had come across three large policies that provided disability insurance if he were unable to work. And he certainly was disabled now. So the brothers favored leaving things as they were, in God's hands as the priest would put it.

Near midnight of that day, the surgeon sorted through his own insurance policies which he had carelessly thrown into a file-cabinet drawer. He found that he too had three large disability policies. He drove home from his office and rousted his wife and five children from bed. As they yawned and blinked in the living room, he announced that they would go on a long trip, one that everyone would enjoy. They all became more wide awake, and soon the house buzzed with the intensity of midday. His wife made up a tray of snacks from a large slab of smoked salmon. She said the priest had brought it by.

I'm Not Beethoven

Can you walk on the water? You have done no better than a straw. Can you fly in the air? You have done no better than a bluebottle. Conquer your heart; then you may be somebody.

Ansari of Herat

A WALK in the snow is as real as repairing the car, a swallow of sour orange juice, sweating out the results of one's X ray reports, changing a diaper, singing a favorite song or signing a death certificate. The crisscrossed tire tracks, the neighbor's dog that skirts us, the distant yellow lights from a house on the hill, the unused stop sign, are all more real than contemplating the chemistry of snow or the physical laws of condensation and freezing.

On this particular walk I am by myself, a walking stick in one hand, a pipe in the other. I cannot force my mind to decelerate and cast off the whirling images of complaints, injustices and failures that walk with me. Aldous Huxley claimed that there should be one sin added to the famous deadly seven: speed. Mind-racing is the form it takes in me. It is as if I cannot stop considering, reconsidering, planning, apologizing. There is a difference between mind-racing and thinking, and I cannot switch from the former to the latter.

Tonight I am stuck on the *whys.* I know that *whys* often have no answers, and when they do, the answers come after long experience and not just from asking the questions. Why are good people often cut down before their time and less worthy ones left alive? Why are some people one hundred percent against abortion, one hundred percent for capital punishment? Why does the AMA wage war against tobacco, which largely kills its users, and take such a meek position against alcohol, which kills its users and so many others? Why does our government court the communist Chinese and detest the communist Russians? Why isn't everyone interested in the sanctuary movement? Why did ABC ever hire Joe Namath for Monday Night Football?

The road moves on up the hill and all is white. Why is it said that no two snowflakes are exactly alike when no one has ever examined them all? A brief relapse into the *whys!* The road is soft under my feet and the snow is dry and fluffy, making my traction good. I stop at the top of the rise. There are no new tracks and the earlier treadmarks are dusted with snow. I puff my pipe into a fiery glow and watch the smoke slide away on the windless night.

Smoke, shadows and clouds are favorite things of mine. Snow belongs there as well. What intrigues me is that all of these are not what they seem to be. If my eye had the resolving power of a telescope or a microscope, smoke, shadows, clouds and snow would look much different to me, when in fact nothing about them had changed.

What does all of this have to do with walking in the snow? I don't know, but I start thinking about it. At least I am off of the *whys.* The woman who wants a miracle pops into my thoughts.

I first saw her several years ago after multiple sclerosis already had a strong hold on her. Her major problems were ambulation and poor balance. She is a woman of devout faith and remains what I consider falsely optimistic about divine healing. She believes in her heart that God will not leave her to such troubles with her broken body if her faith is strong enough. She believes that faith can move mountains and that we have been promised we can do even greater works than our Lord if we but have the faith to do so. Walking is one of these works for her.

However, she has worsened in some ways, and the past several months have been most difficult. She is wheelchair-bound now and it is not clear how much physical improvement she may gain. She was married to a man of little ambition and a wandering nature, and after a time he left her and moved in with the woman across the street. The patient was left with her daughter, the bills and much sadness. If there was a time for her to question religion, it was when all of this happened. She was sustained by the "benefits," as they are called: Social Security, Medicaid and things of that type.

Meanwhile she applied for and acquired a full-time job as a telephone operator at a military base near where she lives, and later remarried, this time to a devoted and kind man who loves her for what she is instead of despising her for what she cannot do. They live in a comfortable house and are both active in their local church.

Recently she was in the hospital again, weaker than ever, and burdened by adjusting to herself as she is. She wants to run on the beach, walk through shopping centers, climb stairs, be trim and well toned. We talked about her life, and she reminded me of what a blessing it is to rise from a chair unaided, drive a car without special attachments and not worry about bladder control. So far, she said, God has not answered her prayers, not because he isn't interested, but because her faith is not strong enough. We discussed miracles, and I asked her which was a greater miracle, the person who is restored to perfect health and lives an ordinary life, or the one who lives an extraordinary life in spite of considerable physical impairments?

"Maybe God decides the form of miracles," I offered.

"Maybe so," she replied, "but I'm not giving up!"

"Beethoven's miracles did not depend upon having his hearing restored."

"I'm not Beethoven," she said.

This night is splendid in its heavy air and newly fallen snow and the sense of wonder that wraps itself around me as I walk. After all, I'm not Beethoven either.

PART TWO

Trade Secrets

Jake and Eph

ON MY father's birthday, September 13, in the year 1955, I waved farewell to my parents and climbed aboard a Greyhound bus in Seattle. I was off to Baltimore to begin my first year at the University of Maryland Medical School. Having never been further east than Idaho, I had no idea of what it was like to bounce along highways so long and empty it seemed like someone was ahead of us making more Montana as we went. The trip took four days and three nights, nonstop. It was the cheapest way to travel, and I was on an austere budget to say the least. Besides, it didn't cost me extra to take all my luggage, including my microscope. When the good-natured black man who loaded baggage in Seattle found out from my mother that I was to be a doctor, he insisted on checking everything through free of charge. Nothing too good for the young doctor.

The heat and humidity of Baltimore was wilting, and I swore I could feel the lurching of the bus for three days after I arrived. I lived with my father's relatives, two unmarried cousins, Charlotte and Elsie, and their aged mother. Their house, far from the medical school, was located just off Belair Road where George Washington once drilled his troops. Each morning I rode the streetcar for almost an hour and disembarked two blocks from the medical school, right in front of Edgar Allan Poe's grave in a small churchyard on the corner.

My clothes had protected me well from the damp chills of the Pacific Northwest but were sadly out of place in Baltimore's tropical heat. Wearing my tweed suit was high punishment indeed, and I had no lightweight woolens. But I wore what I had because I had barely enough money for tuition, let alone a new wardrobe.

Our first-year class contained one hundred students, and I didn't know a one. However, lots of other students were from faraway places as well, and it was easy to make friends. In my innocence I inadvertently joined a Jewish medical fraternity. So did my new friends Bob Holt from West Virginia and Elmer McKay from Colorado. After a brief meeting, the fraternity was declared interdenominational and we all celebrated.

The medical school had a new dean, General William Stone, who had just retired from the army and looked every inch a general. He greeted our class the first morning and made two things clear: first, the faculty did not grade on effort, it graded on performance and second, if we got into any trouble we shouldn't, he would not be a sympathetic listener. He claimed that every student selected was capable of the work required, and his door was always open to discuss anything with any student, except for the disclaimers just mentioned.

The intellectual competition was intense, and I simply didn't have the first-rate study habits that many of the other students did. And I was quite lonely. At the end of the first week, I was ready to quit medical school altogether. It was impossible for me to read, understand and remember pages 12 to 72. I made it to about page 40, and gave up in the wee hours of the morning. If the other students could accomplish this kind of assignment I was badly overmatched, and I might as well take a bus home to Seattle and try to get back my old job in the Sears, Roebuck and Co. warehouse.

The next morning, the professor cheerfully announced that the schedule had a misprint, the assignment was to read pages 12 to 27, not 12 to 72.

I decided to try a bit longer, although the class still seemed formidable to me. In order to stabilize myself, I devised a scheme to give myself encouragement. I knew that only 10 percent of the class was likely to fail, and after scouting around a bit, I picked ten students that I was sure I could outperform academically. As long as none of them quit, I would be all right. Being ninetieth in the class was far better than going home defeated. Besides, I'd heard that the less academic students made more money once they began medical practice.

At night, as I tried for sleep after long hours of study, I frequently thought of the words my old German uncle and enthusiastic supporter, Carl, gave me before I left Seattle: "No matter how discouraged you get, don't quit. Make them throw you out." But for the first few weeks, mentally I had my bags packed.

My room was small but comfortable, and I was treated royally by my wonderful relatives. They encouraged me, fed me, entertained me, loved me, and refused to have anything but complete confidence in me. Such sustenance is rare.

Johns Hopkins Medical School was and still is famous, and I learned that those who attended the University of Maryland Medical School were considered inferior. The best students came to Baltimore to attend Hopkins. Charlotte told me that she understood Maryland was really much better and Hopkins was just riding on its reputation. I didn't believe her, but such affirmation helped.

One of the more bewildering classes that first year was our Saturday-morning conference conducted by the psychiatry department. First there was an hour's lecture by a guest speaker: a sociologist, artist, philosopher, or someone else who seemed to have only the most tangential relationship to medicine. We students wanted to see movies about surgery or the demonstration of a thoracentesis, anything that was truly worth learning. We didn't know any better.

The next two hours were conducted by the head of the department, Dr. Jacob Finesinger, or Jake as we called him, behind his back of course. We were told by the upperclassmen that Jake was a famous psychoanalyst and had studied with Freud himself. I was sure he could see inside me, no matter where I sat.

Jake looked like a doctor, with a large-featured, kind face, heavy gray eyebrows, gray hair straight and a bit mussed. The heavy lines in his face outlined a pleasant smile. He looked as though nothing could faze him. He wore rumpled clothes, and loved to ask us questions we couldn't answer, such as, "How would you treat a patient with a stomach ulcer?" just to see what we would say. Our complaints about his unfair questions did not disturb his equanimity. He just smiled, advised we do our best, and never told us whether or not our answers were correct.

The other teacher at these sessions was an internist, Dr. Ephriam Lisansky, pudgy, arrogant, dressed in tailored suits with a handkerchief in his jacket pocket, immaculately groomed with a rim of dark hair plastered along the sides of his head, and his bald dome shining like a dance floor. He smoked a large-bowled pipe, using it when he spoke as a conductor would a baton. His voice was refined, his diction clear, and he reminded me a little of José Ferrer.

The format of these classes was simple. Jake would interview a patient in front of the class, not a psychiatric patient, but a woman with an uncommon medical disease such as lupus, or a man recovering from a coronary occlusion. Jake never told us what was wrong with the patient. Instead, he had them describe their symptoms, how they felt, something about their lives, what they were worried about, and how they had become ill. Following thirty minutes or so of this, Eph, as we called him among ourselves, came before the class and analyzed the patient from the diagnostic standpoint, baffling us with terms we didn't know, and almost always making the correct diagnosis, confirmed by reading from the patient's chart. *Lupus erythematosis disseminatus* rolled from his tongue like mystical words from heaven. We were watching a medical Sherlock Holmes in action.

We students couldn't figure out what Jake was up to. Eph was the main attraction. At least he talked real medicine. We weren't interested in people, we were interested in fighting disease, and Eph did that with style. But for Jake, the person always seemed more interesting than the disease. Pneumonia was pneumonia and antibiotics could cure that.

Even the most anxious patient, dressed in robe and slippers and accompanied by a nasogastric tube or IV pole, would become absorbed by the kindness and interest of this gentle man who made an interview in front of a hundred medical students intensely personal and dignified. Jake's interest in people was not feigned, and we didn't understand for a long time that he was teaching us about the relationship of people to their illnesses. Without people, there wouldn't be any illnesses. Without people, there would be no need for doctors. If there were no people, then we wouldn't exist either. But he never explained that.

Jake knew what he was doing. As in all true insight, one discovers for oneself what one can never be taught or told because one wouldn't believe it or understand it.

The second year we had the same Saturday-morning format, only now Jake interviewed psychiatric patients, some of whom were severely disturbed and even dangerous. He maintained the same gentle ease, and more than once soon had a frightened, pacing, threatening patient seated next to him and in front of us, talking into the microphone so that we could all hear.

Jake elicited the delusional systems, listened intently to hallucinations, promised to look into patient complaints about how they were treated (and he did).

Healing was more complicated than I had imagined, and I thought how wonderful it would be to talk with someone who was so interested in me and my life. This man used no stethoscope or scalpel. Not that he denigrated medical and surgical care, for he didn't. We found out later that Jake was suffering from cancer of the bowel during the times he was talking to us about patients and patience.

We learned by watching a true dialogue between two people in which neither had to verify their position, nor compete for the upper hand. We also learned that a dying psychoanalyst cared about us, although he never said so, and that caring about each other is the first and foremost step in being a physician.

Physicship, Physicster or Physicker?*

THE word "patient" is derived from the Latin verb *pati* which means "to suffer." If our patients aren't suffering when we start with them, they may well be by the time we finish. Other meanings from the same root word are "long-suffering toward others," "calmly expectant," "persistent," "a sufferer of bodily disease," "under medical treatment," "subjected to supervision or treatment" and "one to whom something is done by an external agent."

"Physician" comes from the word "physic" and a physician is thus "a student of natural science or physics," "a performer of the healing arts, especially in medicine and surgery," "one legally qualified to practice healing arts" and "a healer who cures moral, spiritual, or political infirmities or maladies." "Physic" means "to dose or treat with physic or medicine, especially a cathartic," "natural science," "knowledge of the human body" and "the art of healing." The patient-physician relationship is some combination of the above.

Physicians are like church-goers who participate in the ritual and accept the general principles of the faith but after they go home resume living their lives the way they want to. Or, in our case, in spite of our basic commitments to the

Physicship: a humorous title for a medical authority; *physicster:* a contemptuous term for a medical practitioner; *physicker:* one who administers a physic.

science of it all, we are most influenced in our practices by our experiences, hunches and ideas.

Several years ago I examined a shrivelled, mildly confused and lethargic old man who was hospitalized after his friends found him at home unable to care for himself. His examination, laboratory and basic X-ray studies were unremarkable and there was little history available. I suspected he had a chronic subdural hematoma: a collection of blood between the brain and the skull, compressing the brain. Max, an intense, shaggy house officer, dressed in an open-necked shirt, beads, jeans and sandals, challenged me to defend my diagnosis. Max felt we private doctors needed our skills updated and he resisted most of our ideas and diagnoses. He complained that the old man had no findings to support my diagnosis. I replied that was often the case in subdural hematomas. He wanted references in the medical literature. I offered that I'd seen a lot of subdurals and seldom read about them any more. The only references I came up with were years old. He looked at me with disbelief in his sleep-deprived eyes and I knew I had confirmed his worst suspicions about the ineptitude of private physicians.

Later the same day I discovered a properly referenced note in the patient's chart that soundly criticized my plan to perform a carotid arteriogram; the note advised an injection of dye that would show displacement of the brain if a subdural were present. Max was determined to prove his point. Of course, I couldn't use this case as an example if I hadn't been correct. However, the patient did have a chronic subdural hematoma that a neurosurgeon easily drained through two small holes in the skull, and the patient recovered completely. I tried not to feel superior when I told Max that he was too inexperienced to be writing such strong notes in a patient's chart and by the time he was old enough to do so he'd be smart enough not to.

Not long after that another house officer, Jack, wanted an elective in neurology with me. Jack was intelligent, quiet toward sullen, and not very knowledgeable about neurological matters. But he worked hard and showed unusual compassion toward the afflicted. Jack identified with those who gritted their way through the endless frustrations of ataxias, hemiplegias, aphasias, incontinences of bladder and bowel, and other dysfunctions of the central nervous system. Simpler and less serious disorders interested him little even though I told him I'd seen enough strokes, cerebral hemorrhages and amyotrophic lateral sclerosis to last me a lifetime and I found patients with migraine or cervical strains a welcome relief.

Jack and I had dinner together on the last evening of his elective. We were each to leave on vacation the next morning. He was fascinated by the spectrum of cases we'd seen together and asked repeatedly how I withstood the miseries and sufferings of many of these patients. I can't recall that I gave him a very profound answer, although I did say that I tried to be involved with the patients when I was with them and busy myself in other things when I wasn't. In fact, often I couldn't remember their names once we parted. However, that method was only partially successful in protecting me and sometimes I felt terrible when I couldn't make a diagnosis or didn't have an effective treatment for patients. I tried to find new meanings for my own life through their experiences. Suffering seemed inevitable and necessary although at times simply outrageous. I often wondered how well I would make out if I had to face what some of them faced.

Jack was very interested in what I said and I suggested he read *Man's Search for Meaning* by Viktor Frankl. I complimented him on his interest in more than just disease processes and their treatment, and his genuine concern about others. He acknowledged me with one of his rare smiles and I went off to vacation. That was the last time I saw Jack.

Three weeks later, on my first morning of hospital rounds, my usual postvacation feelings of regret were interrupted by the head nurse who solemnly told me that my intense and compassionate colleague had committed suicide the night of our last dinner. After telling friends he would be out of town for the weekend he consumed a lethal dose of sleeping capsules in the privacy of his locked room. I couldn't ask whether Jack had left a note and I realized I knew nothing of the real torment that he tried to heal by helping others who seemed worse off. I suspect he felt so guilty when he compared himself to those patients that he no longer felt worthy of life. I've always hoped he didn't give me clues about himself which I missed, but I don't know for sure anymore.

Some nights, with rain splattering on the window, embers dying in the Franklin, and John McCormack's beautiful Irish tenor voice melting in the background, I think about Max, who I'm sure went on to professional success, and Jack, who never had the chance. Maybe compassion and empathy will overwhelm us if our intellects are not successful in providing professional detachment. And maybe they won't.

Stethoscope and Goblet

IN SPITE of twelve years of college, medical school and post-graduate training in neurology, and over twenty years of practice in my specialty, I've come to realize that I'm not well educated. Well trained, yes, but not well educated. Education is more than the knowledge and explanation. An example: the scientific basis of brain function as an explanation for human intellect and possibility is not satisfying to me. Neuronal (brain-cell) activity no doubt explains the inner working of these biological computers, but says nothing about the origins and contents of its programs.

Much of what is taken for education is buoyed by principles of problem-solving techniques and statistical verification. According to some, these two attributes, coupled with logical thinking, are the highest human accomplishments and are thus worthy of our most vigorous educational efforts. Of course we need to develop these skills, but not at the price of reducing human emotion and conflict to infantile traumas and poor sportsmanship. Ethereal subjects, lumped under "the arts," are considered to be on a lower level than computer sciences and business practices, on a lower level even than the social sciences. Our educational measuring sticks are performance, grades, diplomas and other indicators that tell us whether or not we are on our way to wealth and elegant homes.

I often wish I were a poet or philosopher seated in a rustic cafe, goblet in hand, surrounded by all manner of good thinkers and creative spirits. We would enter that realm where imagination lives and works of art are created from blending material and spirit. Some call it soul.

Musicians would be held in high esteem. We would sing and dance their compositions. We would meditate on the wind and rain, recite poems and tell stories, and discuss the limitations of all dogma and fixed ideas. Our diplomas and certificates would be hung in the storage room with our coats. There would be room next to the stove for any stray dog that needed warmth. People with heavy hearts would be welcome as long as they didn't ask us how to live their lives.

On the front door would hang a plaque that reads " 'The eye with which you see God and the eye with which he sees you is the same eye.' — Meister Eckhart." Near the stove would be another plaque that reads, "Tat Twam Asi" (you are that), an old Hindu maxim. There would be no clock. Our breath would mingle as would our imaginations, and these would mingle with the heat from the stove and the snores of the dog.

I would keep my stethoscope in my pocket and I would touch it now and then to remind myself that listening is often better than talking. I would never drain my goblet, so I might have a bit left to toast whatever happened next.

When it was my turn, I would tell how as medical students at the University of Washington, which I attended my last two years, we studied human behavior from scientists and ignored poet Theodore Roethke, who taught on the same campus. He knew madness, traveled its terrifying journeys and wrote about it in poetic rather than analytical terms. His poem "In a Dark Time" contains the line, "What's madness but nobility of soul at odds with circumstance?"

When my turn came again, I would describe my Uncle Carl, for whom circumstances permitted only one year of college, who worked as a city engineer and who collected more than four thousand Edison records and twelve thousand books in his small frame house on Queen Anne Hill in Seattle. He knew more about English literature and history as well as classical music than many full-time professionals. He taught me that we are limited only by our curiosity and determination. Great ideas and brilliant minds can survive anything except ignorance and slothfulness.

When we left for our homes, each of us would walk our own path, the night would glisten with special brightness, and we would not feel so bad that none of us is ever educated.

The Role of the Consultant:
Two Cases

CASE One: A simply dressed woman, heavy and about thirty, with tears on her cheeks and alarm in her voice hurried down the hall toward my office clutching her five-year-old son, Jimmie, by the hand. They each took a chair, and after a quick swipe at her nose with a soggy handkerchief she told me the reason for their emergency visit.

The previous evening, she and Jimmie had been home watching television together when he suddenly complained of seeing two pictures instead of one. He tried tilting his head in various directions, squinting and rubbing his eyes, but nothing would improve his vision. She gave him motherly assurance that with a cup of hot chocolate and a good night's sleep he would be better. However, that was not the case. She looked up from her morning coffee and newspaper to see Jimmie weaving down the hall and then collapsing against the frame of the door which led to the kitchen. He held both hands over his eyes and said his double vision was worse then ever. His distraught mother telephoned their family doctor who referred her directly to me.

Her anguish increased as she remembered an uncle who had developed double vision as a symptom of a brain tumor and had died a few months later. Whatever was wrong with

Jimmie, it was not good. That much she knew for sure.

Meanwhile Jimmie sat impassively in his chair, his eyes downcast and a frown on his face. He was small for his age with disheveled straight brown hair and torn jeans. He swung his legs back and forth because his feet didn't reach the floor. Once he looked up at me, then quickly downward again and his frown deepened. He didn't look ill. His mother gained enough control of her anxiety to tell me that Jimmie had no other symptoms, nor any history of recent illness or injury.

She watched intently as I examined Jimmie. When I attempted to check the range of motion of his eyes or their pupillary reaction to light he turned his head away, rubbed both eyes with his hands and whined he couldn't see. His mother pleaded with him to cooperate, but it was no use. He would not be persuaded. Instead he wriggled his tiny body back and forth on the examining table where he sat and steadfastly refused to let me examine his eyes.

I held up a quarter and asked him if he would like it. He slowly slid his hands from his reddened eyes and reached for the money. We struck a bargain by agreeing that in exchange for his performing a few tasks the money was his. Performance before payment, however.

His perfectly coordinated extraocular movements were a strange finding in someone with double vision. Everything about the remainder of his neurological examination was also normal.

His mother gave a plaintive sigh as I shrugged my shoulders and Jimmie asked for his quarter. He stated repeatedly that he saw two fingers side by side when I only held up one no matter what his direction of gaze. I was about ready to give up when I decided to make one more try. I held up two fingers, he saw four, four fingers, he saw eight, five fingers and he saw ten. Now I had him. Next I held up six fingers. Jimmie, well into the spirit of the game, closed his eyes, counted deliberately to himself, then opened his eyes and burst out "twelve" with a triumphant smile on his healthy face.

Meanwhile, his mother's tears evaporated, her pupils dilated and her eyelids narrowed. I winked at her to soften her anger as I handed Jimmie the quarter and suggested she and I adjourn to the next room where we could talk privately. She was an odd mixture of rage and relief. After staring down at the floor for a moment, her sense of humor took over. I explained that in my specialty, with all its miserable diseases, I was relieved to find a little fakery now and then and that she and Jimmie might do well to consider themselves blessed.

But what really upset her was that several months earlier she had taken Jimmie to see a vascular specialist because his feet suddenly turned blue. And she knew from another uncle who had to have his leg amputated after his foot turned blue that this was no laughing matter. It turned out Jimmie had waded in mud puddles in his new blue tennis shoes and blue socks, hidden the wet shoes and socks when he came in for lunch and appeared for his hot soup with deep blue feet.

I told her I hoped Jimmie didn't go into politics.

Case Two: One evening I was summoned to the Intensive Care Unit of a large local hospital to see a strange case of unexplained postoperative agitation. The patient had had a large abdominal aortic aneurysm resected earlier in the day by a skilled and experienced vascular surgeon. There were no particular surgical or anesthetic problems and the patient had been placed in the ICU more as a precaution than a necessity.

Two or three hours after his arrival in the ICU, he suddenly began to react to efforts to move him or change his position by vigorously twisting and writhing in his bed. Increased sedation didn't help. An oral airway was taped into place and his hands and feet restrained. He would drop off to sleep only to become unmanageable whenever the nurses attended him. Arterial blood gases were checked and re-checked since some thought hypoxia the most likely diagnosis, but the results were within the normal range. Oxygen administered empirically was of no benefit. Electrolytes, glucose, calcium and numerous other blood studies were also normal. Idiosyncratic drug reaction, postoperative intra-abdominal bleeding and early sepsis were all considered but could not be proven. Finally, someone suggested a neurological consultation.

I was called in as a last resort, and no one, including me, was confident of any success. As usual, all the obvious tests had been run, which left me to suggest a lumbar puncture and maybe a check for urinary porphobilinogen. The head nurse, a concerned and efficient woman, suspected acute viral encephalitis, which was not a bad guess.

The patient slept soundly and looked quite peaceful as I approached his bed. I shook him. He slept on. I shook him harder and called his name. He opened his heavy eyelids and looked up at me. Suddenly he arched his back, flung his head from side to side and struggled to free his hands and feet. Soon the medication overtook him again and he fell asleep. Except for his agitated arousal responses his neurological examination was entirely unremarkable. I confessed I was baffled.

Outside his room, I had a brief conversation with his worried wife and could not obtain any information about his medical or personal life that helped to explain his condition. I muttered a few neurological terms, admitted my confusion and recommended a lumbar puncture. She agreed although she was skeptical that the results would be helpful to her husband who'd already had a hard day.

Back at the bedside of the patient, I helped the nurses untie his left hand and foot and roll him onto his right side with his back toward me. He struggled against us and as I reached over to pull his knees up toward his chest a bit, the obscure became obvious. Sticking in his left buttock was a hypodermic needle which had become detached from its syringe during the administration of postoperative pain medication. Every time the poor man moved, he jabbed himself. I removed the needle, gave up the lumbar puncture and rolled him back over. His agitation disappeared and he fell into a deep and no doubt relieved sleep.

He recovered uneventfully.

Toward the New Year

DURING the busyness of the holiday season I have come to my favorite place, my refuge: a cabin on the beach of Marrowstone Island. I left home at eight-thirty this morning, drove from Bainbridge Island to the Lofall ferry, crossed Hood Canal and drove on to my destination, arriving about ten-thirty. Because I was alone in my truck I let my mind fill with topics, ideas, admonishments and inspirations aroused by frost on the road, sparse winter trees, shaggy horses scattered in brown fields, the Olympic Mountains blazing like white gods in the morning sunlight and the anticipation of a day to myself. I thought, "If I can't write today, I never will be able to."

After I parked my pickup truck along the road I carried my needs for the day, including a notebook and a tape recorder complete with classical-music tapes, down the walk and I unlocked the cabin door. The cold inside the cabin was like doom, and the eeriness of a place exactly as I'd left it a few weeks earlier reminded me of how static my life can be. Soon I dismissed that idea and busied myself replacing blown fuses, turning on the water pump and building a fire in the stone fireplace. The room slowly filled with smoke as the heavy damp air in the chimney refused to let new smoke enter. However, fresh spirit always wins out if it is persistent enough, so I added wood until a dancing, friendly fire began to warm the room and the smoke ascended as it should.

When dry hemlock burns it becomes a cheerful blaze that gives off loud crackles, bright sparks and a pleasant aroma before dissolving into smoke and rising up the chimney into the atmosphere. Such a pleasant fate. Little does the hemlock realize its potential for warmth, light, fragrance and travel. If the hemlock can do that, think what we humans can do. Or, as with hemlock trees, we may fall down from our own weight and rot on some forest floor.

While the fire warms the cabin I walk in the woods across the road. They are wet and soggy with decaying leaves. Many trees have broken off during recent violent storms and their parts lie randomly about. Other trees have fallen only partially over, lodging in the strong branches of their immobile neighbors, probably without permission to do so. I walk on into the deserted meadow where blackberry vines catch my boots. Deer trails meander through the brown dead grass. The winter sun takes on the darkening day but is losing to the heavy clouds carried by a freshening wind.

Back inside the cabin I fix a lunch of dried onion soup, cheese, crackers and tea. I wish I hadn't decided on such a Spartan existence for today. As I eat at the kitchen table, I can see across Scow Bay to Indian Island, which is part of the Trident Submarine Base. The stands of fir trees along its beach attempt to hide the enormous destructiveness housed in concrete buildings beyond. William Stafford, one of our greatest contemporary poets, and I stood on the deck of this cabin last summer and stared at the same innocent-appearing shoreline. He tightened his lined face and said in his soft, quiet voice, "They say it is our country but we can't go there.

They say what they do is for us, but they won't tell us what it is."

With my walk accomplished, my lunch concluded, the cabin warm and Schubert filling the air, I search for the impulse to write by remembering that Giuseppe Verdi composed the entire opera *Rigoletto* in forty days and thus I can surely write one short prose piece in an afternoon. My inner critic loves to hear me say those things, and he is ruthless in his ridicule. No thoughts go together and soon I have a stack of torn sheets of paper lying next to me. I decide relaxation is what I need. I retire to a comfortable chair and start to read from Aldous Huxley's *Perennial Philosophy*. In a short time I am fast asleep.

My dreams are troubled. I don't bother to wake up in order to record them. They give me a clear message: I am best at causing trouble, and if I know what is good for me I'll stay in line. The world around me knows best. When I wake with a sore neck from sleeping in an uncomfortable position, I look across to Indian Island again and I know that much of the world around me is suspect as far as integrity and responsibility are concerned.

The graceful winter twilight slides in and the clouds seem frozen in bitterly cold formations. If I could see what they see, I might better understand the world and know more clearly what I should do. I recall a speaker at one of those easy-to-forget meetings on health care who stated that twenty percent of the American people did not have adequate health insurance and as a result were denied proper medical care. My silent reaction at that time was to wonder which group might be healthier: the eighty percent who did or the twenty percent who didn't. That's a hard question to ask myself and I don't think I'll give a public answer.

Dusk gathers. Mergansers, bluebills, grebes and other sea birds and ducks huddle together in small clumps scattered across the flat bay. The tide has receded and the barnacled beach is exposed. Outside my window heavy fir limbs rustle and are quiet. All is quiet. This day has nearly passed and all creatures prepare for night. Another year has also nearly passed and the nature of mankind has not noticeably improved.

Mankind still talks mostly about survival: of recession, of despair, of nuclear war, of each other. Me? I want to live in a world of new experiences where things are not all planned or explained and thus I will have many more discoveries as I find my way through this next year. What greater gift could I give myself? And it is mine if I want it to be.

The fire dies. The night is dense black with no visible stars. I put my papers and books back into their case, collect tapes and recorder, turn off the pump in the well-house, close up the cabin, walk out in a fine refreshing rain and climb into my truck. I drive home in the darkness, but I have enough light to see where I am going and that is all I ask.

Sons of Osler

EACH of the following characterizations is based upon a composite of incidents, experiences and conversations I've come across in my years of medical practice, during which time I have served on many committees, such as utilization review, cost containment, malpractice evaluation, grievance and medical standards.

There is in human matters always a little larceny in the heart. Sometimes a lot of larceny. Business, whether capitalist or communist, depends upon it. It is one of the major reasons that we have such a complicated legal system, which must decide by one means or another which larceny is the lesser in a specific case. Within the medical profession matters are no different. We have various means of deciding what constitutes "reasonable care and fees." That is no easy matter, for it is difficult to take into account all the variables in skills, dedication and efficiency among physicians. And generally we make no effort to examine the relative values of services and procedures which, it seems to me, have come about largely by accident and are thus without any consistent pattern.

I offer here a few composites of physicians who are outside the mainstream of medical and surgical practice.

They may be opportunists who know how to work the system — and do. Or they may be beyond their best years and yet unwilling to quit, even though their skills are declining. Some of these examples will hit painfully close to us all. Most of these concerns are ones of degree. I write in the first person to make it harder for both the writer and readers to put distance between themselves and the narratives.

Finally, lest women feel slighted by the title, "Sons of Osler" simply sounds better than "Androgynous Offspring of the Greater Healer." Also, since some descriptions will include actions of female physicians, and since I do not wish to point my finger at anyone specific, I can more safely proceed.

I

The big hand has joined the little hand straight up on my antique German clock, reminding me that it is time for a suitable portion of fifteen-year-old scotch-on-the-rocks before I am picked up by my friend for our daily golf game. I spend a lot of time here in Arizona far from the unremitting drizzle of Puget Sound, but my heart is still up there in the low-lying Pacific Northwest clouds. It should be! That place has been awfully good to me.

It was over thirty years ago when I started my practice in Seattle. I soon realized that I did not want any of this "bust-your-britches-and-never-get-paid" type of medicine my uncle practiced in the Midwest. If I had wanted to be a missionary I would have gone to Africa.

My principles are simple: there are always people who want certain care and are willing to pay to get it. If they don't get it from me, they will get it from someone else. Either way they get it. My way, we both get it, if you get what I mean.

So I found my way into the weight-reduction business —
bariatrics they call it now. This was a field with no emergencies and lots of money to be made. My only limitation was
that I was a little porky myself, so I bought loose-fitting
smocks for me and small gowns for the patients.

Fat people know one thing that some of you might think
about: most doctors don't like to treat obesity. It isn't as
exciting as treating sub-acute bacterial endocarditis.
Health-insurance carriers will not cover treatment for obesity
and the patients have to spend their own money. So why
shouldn't they come to someone who specializes in their
problem and caters to their needs?

Most fat people are ashamed they are fat. Their feelings
are easily hurt. Call them stupid and they may get mad, but
call them fat and they are reduced to stunned silence or an
embarrassing acknowledgement that you are right. That's
because it is harder to hide bulk than wicked thoughts. They
are impulsive about weight loss, a subject that occupies a
great deal of their thinking. Frequently they change from one
program to another and want the latest fad. Witness the
number of diet books for sale.

Furthermore, they believe in two irrefutable tenets.
First, their disorder is glandular; and second, most of their
excess weight is fluid retention. Overeating is a result, not a
cause. So treatment is simple: Give one pill for the glands,
one for the fluids and one for the supression of appetite along
with a specific diet and lots of vitamins. (If one of my patients
ever developed a vitamin deficiency it would be a miracle.)

Sometimes I get criticized by my colleagues, but I also
get a lot of patients who are dissatisfied with these same
colleagues. To be sure, I can't prescribe Class II drugs any-

more. Too free with the dexedrine, I was told. Of course fat people can buy booze, which isn't good for them, and no one arrests the liquor-store clerk. Nevertheless, they won't allow me to prescribe dexedrine, which does help them lose weight. So I suffice by giving patients a lot of fluids along with their diuretics, which keeps them busy.

The righteousness of the medical society comes down on me at times. Some members love to investigate my practice. It makes them feel socially responsible — "accountability," they call it. I always manage to be unavailable when I'm supposed to appear before one of their committees, and soon I receive another ambiguously worded threatening letter. When they get too close I have my lawyer goose them a little, and they huddle together like a herd of sheep to try to figure out what they should do next. The law is on my side — "due process," they call it. But in the end, they don't have any stomach for the fight. (That's a bad pun from a fat-doctor.) My patients never complain about me and they are proud that I don't give in. Being a scapegoat can be a great advantage if you play it right.

While I'm down here, my patients are up there eating themselves into shape, so to speak. Well, it's been nice talking with you — continuing medical education, they call it. Too bad my wife, Betty — no, wait, she was my last one — Mildred, I mean, couldn't be here. There's my ride. You can find your own way out. Remember, eat hearty.

II

Looking at the overall scheme of things, I'm surprised at how many issues are resolved in courtrooms. I've been a judge for a long time and a trial lawyer before that, and through it all I've learned that there comes a time when someone must decide a dispute or arrive at a judgment. The courtroom is well suited for criminal cases, business disputes and other kinds of grievances. The cases that seem to fit the least well into this framework are those involving personal injury.

In almost no other type of case is the outcome so dependent upon expert testimony, which is based upon the concept of reasonable medical certainty. That is to say, it is more likely than not that the patient's injuries, symptoms and permanent disabilities, if any, are due to someone else's negligence. There are really only two things to fight about: namely, whose fault is it and how much is it worth? The jury decides both of these issues although they are never told what the plaintiff would have been willing to settle for rather than go to trial, nor what the defense has offered as a settlement. Witnesses are under oath and attorneys aren't. As the judge I can only instruct the jury in the law, and I'm not supposed to help guide their verdict. If one attorney is doing a lousy job with a witness, I can't intervene and ask the pertinent questions myself. The jury is on its own.

Thus the jurors must hear and evaluate the expert testimony for themselves and obviously no lawyer puts a witness on the stand who is detrimental to the client's case. Expert medical testimony isn't always reliable, as the following examples will show.

I recently heard a case in which a woman was suing for damages to her neck following a rear-end collision in which her car suffered ninety-six dollars' damage. Expert testimony on her behalf, in this instance chiropractic — but I've heard MDs and DOs say similar things — pontificated as to why she had required three thousand dollars' worth of chiropractic care during the two and one-half years since the accident, during which time she had not improved sufficiently to return to work as a clerk in a department store. Furthermore, the expert anticipated several thousand dollars' more treatment would be necessary to correct her misaligned spine, and even then it was doubtful whether or not she could ever be gainfully employed again. I wanted to tell the jury I'd never heard of a case in which someone stayed off work for long or required much treatment after they had injured their neck skiing or falling down the stairs on their own, with no liable third party.

All too often I find "advocate witnesses," medical experts of one kind or another who always represent the same point of view, plaintiff or defense. Some plaintiff attorneys know physicians who will always find something wrong with their client and some defense lawyers know physicians who never seem to find much wrong with anyone. The jury members usually don't know this and they are often in a poor position to evaluate expert medical testimony. They ask, "How is it that two qualified medical experts can arrive at exactly the opposite conclusions?" Of course, there are honest differences of opinion by reputable witnesses. But if the experts can't agree, how can the jury? The jury also doesn't realize that the reason the case hasn't been settled prior to trial is because there is conflicting evidence and/or expert opinion. If both sides agreed, no trial would be necessary.

Even more destructive, malicious and frankly disreputable witnesses are those who present themselves as the world's authority in some minor field, often toxicology or pharmacology. They usually come from large institutions or universities and bring along impressive credentials, bibliographies and boxes of slides. Their testimony may be difficult to offset, even if it is ludicrous, for no one is as sure of himself as the self-appointed expert. Just because someone has written a lot about a subject doesn't indicate scholarship or scientific expertise. It may mean that the easiest way to become an expert in a given field is to be only in that field. Most of these experts are expensive and often quite effective. I recall one case where an enterprising young defense attorney impeached such an expert by demonstrating that the witness had presented conflicting testimony in a previous case. I enjoyed excusing the witness.

In one case it came out that the expert had appeared in trials as a defense witness several times a month for many years and had never yet appeared on behalf of a plaintiff. In another case, a physician was shown to set his witness fee according to how successful he had been in increasing the size of the award. The lawyers who used him regularly must have known this and approved. In another instance, a clinical psychologist testified at great length about the permanent brain damage a plaintiff suffered from a head injury in an automobile accident. Imagine the jury's surprise when it came out that she never struck her head. Whether the psychologist knew that or not I don't know, but in either event neither he nor his tests could be considered reliable. No doubt he continues to testify with all his statistics, charts and polysyllabic words.

Some of this testimony is so predictable that we judges should receive compensation for the pain and suffering we endure while listening.

If I may be expansive for a moment, the principles of advocacy represent one of civilization's greatest advances. No more can a capricious king or paranoid duke separate your head from your body because of some petty crime you committed. But we have moved so far in the direction of following procedure and rules that we now have non-experts decide issues which I think should be decided by experts. I'm afraid we've become more interested in the game than the truth.

III

On a wet October evening twenty-five years or so ago, I sat restlessly in my one-story medical-office building and watched maple leaves plummet through flickering lights to the pavement. A prominent local elected official had called me earlier in the day and pleaded that we meet privately as soon as possible. So I closed my clinic early, and after the staff had left I let myself back in. He was later than he had promised but I was sure he would show. Though he hadn't revealed the nature of his business with me I knew what he wanted.

Soon car lights flashed across the parking lot as a large, dark sedan pulled in and stopped. Three people, bent against the rain, splattered through the puddles on the asphalt and hurried through the unlocked oak door into my waiting room. They spoke in low and muffled tones which I could not decipher. I am sure I looked tired and dedicated with my carelessly rolled-up sleeves and loosened necktie as I turned my swivel chair and called them into my office.

He was even more arrogant than I had remembered him from his last political campaign as he pointed each of them to a chair and neglected introductions. He was handsome in a superficial, theatrical fashion, and his wife was silent and trim without pretense. Her eyes were firm and large and she looked directly at me without apology or fear. With those eyes, I would have voted for her any time. The patient, a frightened girl of about sixteen, sat between her parents and unconsciously leaned toward her mother and away from her father. Despite her youth she had that certain mystery that beautiful women always have and that her mother didn't. I could imagine that men and boys alike had been trying to seduce her for several years. At least one had been successful; she was eight weeks pregnant.

Her father stared over my head at the wall, focusing on a painting of an ancient Indian woman with the lines of eternal persecution and survival on her face. He implied, although never actually said, that his daughter had been raped. Like a lot of politicians he had his particular version of the truth welded into his concretized view of life. His wife and daughter looked relieved that I was not interested in his narrative. But I didn't interrupt. At last he summoned the courage to ask if I would perform an abortion on his daughter. He carefully avoided revealing how he knew about that side of my practice and I didn't ask. I was a hard-working general doctor and only a carefully selected few knew of my abortionist activities.

He explained how politically catastrophic public knowledge of his daughter's pregnancy would be to him. The very foundation of his administration was a crackdown on crime, especially sexual deviation, prostitution and promiscuity. *Abortion* was a word he'd never mentioned in polite company. For him the sanctity of motherhood, family, home and baseball was what makes America great. I didn't disagree with that position, except I knew that even the most well-intentioned and forthright people make mistakes through their own negligence or carelessness, and I've never held that against them. I always thought that a girl or woman shouldn't have to complete pregnancy if she didn't want to, provided it could be safely terminated. Not sentiment on my part, just a way to help.

He stumbled on, trying to find that particular combination of words which would arouse my sympathy for him. The combination didn't exist. In desperation he offered to meet any price I could name, within reason of course. I've never known what that means. My standard fee was modest even though I risked my license every time I went through this. Besides, he was not to be trusted. If he had been the one who was pregnant I could have easily refused.

After a few minutes I interrupted by asking his daughter whether she wanted to be relieved of her pregnancy. He tried to answer for her but I put my index finger to my lips as I studied her face and ignored his. She nodded as color filled her cheeks. Did she understand how this would be done? She shook her head, watching my face intently. I could spend my life forgiving her.

He was livid with the anger of one who must always make the decision whether or not it is his to make. If she had said not to go through with it, I wouldn't have. His was a hatred of what he couldn't understand and never wanted to. A broad, unfocused hatred from a position of masculine superiority dependent upon fragmented facts and never altered by intuition or love. Tolerance was the best he would ever manage.

The girl rested in a pleasant medicinal stupor after I finished. Her mother had remained at her side, adding calmness and confidence by her presence. I knew from those eyes that she didn't approve and would never have had an abortion herself. Yet I realized that her love accepted what must be done. And we both knew that although her daughter had been saved from the burdens of motherhood in the near future, her life would never be the same again. Her innocence was gone forever. Her mother thanked me with a soft touch on my arm and a sad smile that indicated that I would never see either of them again. I didn't.

Meanwhile, her father sat in the outer room listening to the radio, puffing on an expensive pipe and periodically inquiring how much longer we would be. Later, when they left my office, he reminded me of the necessity of strict secrecy and he gave me two hundred dollars extra. Later, I gave it to charity.

Several years after that, two important events happened in my life. First, I was forced to retire from medical practice after I spent two years in a federal penitentiary for income-tax evasion. I never knew how to list those clandestine earnings on my tax return. And I never knew for sure who turned me in for audit.

The second important event was the legalization of abortion. What I had done for years at great risk and with severe public disapproval as another form of murder, was now perfectly legal, encouraged and even covered by health insurance.

I'm still not impressed much by public morality. If you add up the issues of abortion and capital punishment, it comes out like this: Liberals can kill all of them they want to before they are born, but once they are born they get to stay no matter how treacherous and destructive they become. Conservatives won't kill any of them before they are born, but once they are born, they can be done away with if they become undesirable.

Along the Way

I WAS twenty-nine when I started practice, and by my early thirties I was rolling. I had no idea of what my income as a neurologist might be, but it was bound to be a lot of money to the son of a detective sergeant. Not that I was rich, but it seemed like it because I was thirty years old before I made enough money to support my family.

After a few years I prided myself in being able to afford expensive clothes, an elegant house and new cars, things I'd only dreamed about during those long years when we drank powdered milk because it was cheaper and going to a movie was a big evening.

With money came what I thought was prestige. In 1965 I paid cash for a power lawn mower. I told my wife that the clerk must have been impressed when I forked out two fifties and a twenty after announcing, "I'll just pay for it."

We could now afford a house of the quality I used to admire from afar when as a boy I delivered flowers from florist shops during the holidays. I was the swamper, the one who rode with a driver, pulled out the next package and ran it up to the door while the driver waited. I remembered Christmas parties during the forties, held in gorgeous brick houses with huge lawns and expensive cars parked along the streets in front. And the elegantly dressed people visible through the windows as I stood in the cold night rain and waited for someone to answer the door, take the wrapped plant, and, if I was lucky, give me a quarter tip.

I remembered the truck drivers loading their rigs in the unheated garage where the packages were sorted according to areas of the city and then routed in the order in which they could be delivered most efficiently. A good route planner was as essential as gasoline. These men, mostly earthy veterans of World War Two, passed around a bottle of whiskey wrapped in the brown bag it came in, each man wiping the bottle top with his sleeve, saying "Here's mud in your eye," and taking a long slow sip.

I remembered my father who delivered flowers during the holidays in order to supplement his income; policemen didn't make much money in those days. He let me start as his swamper when I was ten. I remembered my mother ready with a hot meal when my father and I finally got home, and my younger brother wanting to know how much money I'd made that day. We often worked twelve to fifteen hours a day during the few days before Christmas. When I got too tired I fell asleep in the Chev station wagon with wooden sides, and my father ran the stairs himself.

In college I continued to work, unloading trucks at night and washing them on Saturdays. In addition I worked in warehouses and as a clerk for Sears, Roebuck and Company. For a time I sold paint, even mixed colors together to produce new shades and tints, some of which, according to others, were spectacular: I am partially colorblind. People who have normal color vision seem fascinated by those of us who don't. They often ask what color I see when I look at dark red or green. Of course I have no answer. I tell them they should be glad that I am not emperor of a world where my word would be final. I would decree that there is no maroon because I have looked and cannot find it. The red-tailed hawk would be renamed the brown-tailed hawk.

It is that looking and being unable to see that requires so much trust between my patients and myself. Once I cared for an elderly Norwegian man whose accent was as dense as lutefisk. He suffered from unexplained episodes of delirium, sometimes leading to temporary coma. My evaluation included all the diagnostic tests and medical treatments I could come up with. Nothing helped.

After several weeks of trying I was embarrassed when he returned to report my latest plan had also failed. I was candid with him: I didn't know the answer and I was firing in the dark. He took me by the arm and said that he knew I was a good doctor and he was sure that sooner or later I would figure it out. Meanwhile, he and his wife agreed that they would just have to wait.

Then I got lucky. He was in the hospital for further studies when he suffered one of his attacks. His wife summoned the nurse and demanded that her husband be given black coffee because that brought him out of these attacks at home. When the nurse returned with the coffee, his wife added several packets of sugar to it and, after rousing him with loud words of Norwegian encouragement, forced him to swallow it. Within minutes he was wide awake and none the worse for wear. His wife explained that Norwegians had to have their coffee. I had missed the point in the history about him recovering after drinking coffee. My mistake.

I anxiously waited for his next attack, which came two days later. This time I had a blood-sugar drawn before the sugared coffee was given and found that he was severely hypoglycemic. The cause: an insulinoma, a rare insulin-secreting tumor of the pancreas that periodically discharged excessive amounts of insulin, lowering his blood sugar so much that his brain function was impaired. When I told him and his wife that it was the sugar and not the coffee that brought him around, she was skeptical.

After the tumor was surgically removed, his attacks disappeared. When it was apparent that he was cured, he came by my office, pumped my hand with one huge fisher-man's paw while patting me on the back with the other one. He said he knew all along that I'd figure out his problem sooner or later. He winked as he said that his wife still thought it was the coffee.

Sometimes I do better when I follow my hunches, especially with those patients who have been evaluated by other competent neurologists with the answer still not forth-coming. Soon after I started practice, a family brought their nine-year-old daughter from another part of the state. Her problem was a twisted neck, with her chin pulled to the right and pointed in the air. They had seen several other neurologists, and no one could make a specific diagnosis. My partner was well known as a diagnostician and thus they had sought him out. He wasn't sure what to make of her and asked me to take a look.

Nothing much about the history made sense, and the angle at which she carried her head did not remind me of any neurological syndrome I could think of. As I palpated her neck muscles, the tension at which they were held varied. On a hunch I took her head between my hands and moved it into a normal position. I told her that she would be more comfortable if she would carry her head that way instead of keeping it tilted at such an angle. She said it did feel better, and she moved it around in all directions. She was cured. We adults stood by as amazed witnesses to "the laying on of hands." There may have been a Freudian explanation for a girl with a twisted neck, but I never searched it out. To find that such a troublesome problem was symptom-corrected, and to learn that she had none of the dreaded diseases of the brain satisfied me. We never saw her again.

I recall another experience with a female patient that did not work out so well for me. One day I was asked to examine a twenty-two-year-old girl with a bizarre hairdo who was admitted to the hospital because of "seizures." As I stood at the side of her bed and watched her flailings, I was sure she was putting us on in order to receive drugs. Intravenous Valium is one of the standard treatments for repetitive seizures, and people who like to take drugs usually love Valium. She had already received two doses.

She writhed, jerked and moaned and kept her eyes closed as she shook her head back and forth. One of the telltale signs of fakes is that they never hurt themselves during their attacks. That was the case with her. I decided to call her bluff. I leaned over her bed to get as close as possible to her without getting conked and I spoke in my best professional voice.

She ignored me. Next I turned to threats. I told her that if she kept this up, we would all leave the room and she would get nothing to eat or drink. The two nurses in attendance, who were worn out from their efforts to control this young woman, nodded their heads in approval. Again no response, although another telltale sign of fakery revealed itself. She stopped to rest when she got tired. Whatever tiny doubts I may have had regarding the nature of her so-called seizures were dissolved. She was a pure phony, and I told her so in clear and unmistakable terms.

Her right arm shot through the side rails and her clenched right fist struck me right between my front pants pockets. I did some moaning and writhing of my own. She stopped, glared at me and resumed her choreography. I smiled as I looked to the nurses for sympathy. They were biting their tongues to keep straight faces.

After a bit my pain subsided and I felt well enough to leave the room. One of the two nurses walked down the hall with me. As we passed the main desk she announced to the head nurse that I had proved the patient was a fake and could be discharged as soon as someone came for her. The head nurse asked how I had done that. "Trade secret," I replied. I could only imagine the high hilarity when the two nurses described my technique during the nursing report held at the change of shifts.

Each of these three patients added to the fabric of what I am and what I do. The hardest lesson of all for me is the constant reminder that I can only learn from ignorance. As I've grown older, I've learned not to trust myself when I can't smell a little horse manure on one boot. Sometimes the odor is much more apparent to others than it is to me. Sometimes it isn't, and that's when the greatest danger lives.

Lunch at the Plaza

WE ARE seated in groups of eight at round tables in a local hotel. I am participating in a conference on health-care delivery systems. It is a beautiful spring day and my impulse is to go outside and walk. I've been living in Seattle for almost a week because of a ferry strike, and it's a hundred-mile drive to my home on Bainbridge Island and back again.

At night, I sleep at my mother's home in north Seattle in a bedroom I've not slept in since I was fourteen years old. Memories of being a lonely sophomore at Lincoln High School, which had fifteen hundred or more students in those days, wander through my twilight as I drift off to sleep. Many of my father's things are in this room — as this is where he lived during the final portion of his life. Most of his usable clothes have been distributed throughout the family, but an assortment of things remains.

This morning I select from a large rack of old neckties. I pick a broad one with lots of stripes. Being partially color-blind, I'm not too sure what I am looking at, but I figure it's hard to go wrong with a solid light blue shirt and suit. My mother tells me I look fine. She always says that. I ask my oldest son, who is living there with his wife temporarily while they get settled in new jobs. He gives me a grin and says, "If that's what you like." We both laugh, and then he tries to reassure me that the tie is really quite nice, but he can't stop laughing. I wear it anyway.

Our lunch arrives and I am seated next to a man from San Francisco I met four years ago at a similar conference. We remember each other because of our mutual interest in opera, and we have a fine time comparing performances we've seen and heard, exchanging anecdotes about singers. We discuss and debate the merits of Pavarotti, Domingo and Carreras — we both love tenors — and agree that Jussi Bjoerling, who died in 1960 at the age of forty-nine, was the best of them all.

Our conversation ends and our attention is directed toward the luncheon speaker. He has come from a college across the state where he teaches speech and motivational techniques. He is trim, well groomed and has a clear delivery and uses no notes. He engages as many of the audience in eye contact as he can and comments on their reactions to what he says as he watches their faces. His opening jokes are pretty stale, a mistake we've all made. He promises to talk for only thirty or forty minutes, and his general topic is about success, failure, motivation and efficiency.

He describes a beautiful and intelligent girl whom many would envy, whose self-esteem is so low that she is afraid to give a speech in front of his class. Next he describes a man whose face was severely disfigured by burns requiring multiple surgeries, which still left terrible scars, and who went on to become a source of inspiration and joy for many as a singer.

Then a sequence of techniques about how to deal with stress, organize the day, and never handle any piece of paperwork more than twice. And a particularly good suggestion for terminating long and irrelevant telephone conversations — hang up in the middle of your own sentence. The caller will think you've been cut off because no one ever hangs up on themselves.

Considering the formidable task of holding the attention of an audience that has already listened to speeches for three hours and whose stomachs are full of chicken salad, rolls and sherbet, he makes out pretty well.

Next, the speaker moves into the meat of his speech, and although I cannot recall the exact sequence of what he said, my description is generally accurate.

He gave us examples of people who were unbelievably successful in salesmanship: a man who made two hundred thousand dollars a year selling Chevrolets in Detroit no matter what the market conditions, another man who sold a billion dollars' worth of life insurance in a single year, and some enormously successful realtors and developers. Each of these persons has foolproof sales techniques. These include making it appear the sales commission is unimportant to them, or conveying a sense of love and concern for their client, while memorizing the names of all the children and even the dog. The car salesman has a prospective buyer sit in a new car, for its aroma is seductive and increases the desire to own the car.

My natural wariness of sales techniques in general and inspirational speeches in particular is reinforced because I have heard no consideration given to any motive except the sale. For example, how many people needed or could afford those Chevrolets? Or life insurance policies? Perhaps the speaker, professional though he is, didn't allow enough time to cover some of these other matters. Maybe the scope of his talk was too large. However, his clear emphasis was on personal success, defined as completing the sale. He made no mention of responsibility to the customer. It is similar to celebrities advertising products and services only because they are well paid to do so, not because they have any conviction or even any experience with whatever they are selling. As we who ride buses know, some deodorants are much better than others regardless of who advertises them.

To my mind, much of public relations and image-building is convincing people of significant advancement or improvement when that is not what will happen. Carefully designed newspaper or television releases call attention to the supposed uniqueness or superiority of a product or service.

We must be careful not to let this happen in medicine, and there are signs that it is.

I wonder what would happen if I organized myself to become an efficient salesman in neurology and developed my staff and program to maximize patient participation for my financial advantage. I could give a family rate on electro-encephalograms, or a week at Ocean Shores Resort for the patient who improved the most this month from his or her cervical strain. After a certain number of office visits, the patient would receive a free month's supply of medication. Anyone who brought in five new patients would receive a perfectly focused lateral skull X ray of themselves suitable for framing. Soon, I would be interviewed on a local television news program. After a while I could organize an overseas tour of medical facilities for those who met certain financial criteria, reserving a healthy cut of the money for myself.

Now I don't want any of you to worry. I am too lazy to ever attempt such an ambitious effort. Besides, the only one who makes any money on my investments is the one who sells them to me. I, along with a bunch of other suckers, am still making payments on a farm that is underwater every time the river rises. The view from my riverfront property is of a dike. We picked up this "choice acreage," sight unseen, ten years ago through a company long since shut down by the Securities and Exchange Commission. We believed the brochure. If any of you are interested in buying this land, give me a call. I guarantee you will be as close to the water as it is possible to get.

My Turn

FOR me the times of learning and insight come when they are least expected. Each day there are experiences that flit by like a hummingbird caught in a sidelong glance and then gone, and I'm not sure if I saw it or imagined it. But either way, I become aware of what I was not thinking about. This is one of the considerable gifts of humanity, to recall or imagine something other than what seems overwhelming at the moment.

I

My first experience as a surgical patient came about from my own carelessness. My oldest son, fourteen at the time, and I were duck hunting on a pond near Sequim. The use of the pond was leased to a group of us, and we had an informal gun club. One morning, Kurt and I were standing near our truck, drinking hot chocolate and complaining about the lack of migrating ducks. Suddenly six or seven dipped in over the tree and lit in the pond.

I offered to sneak around to the back of the pond while

Kurt crawled close to the dike. When he was in position, I would flush the ducks over him and he should get good shots. But the ducks spooked out the far end of the pond long before I could get into position behind them. Our plan failed and no other ducks were visible in the quiet blue sky. I waded across the pond in my hip boots and both of us admired three white swans that beat their way over our heads. I intended to climb a barbed wire fence that stood along the edge of the dike. After I had handed Kurt my unloaded gun through the fence, he started to warn me, too late. I climbed the three bottom strands, caught my boot in the fourth and fell over the top headfirst onto the soggy pasture below the level of the dike, a distance of several feet.

I was knocked out for a moment. When I came around, Kurt was a mixture of concern and laughter. "You should have seen yourself," he said. My headache was intense, and I couldn't move my right arm. I was terrified that I had broken my neck. If I were a quadriplegic I'd just as soon be finished off right here in the pasture. I could never face living that way.

I palpated the spines of my cervical vertebrae and there were no tender places. I palpated my right shoulder, and felt the separation of clavicle from acromion. I moved my legs without difficulty, and my head cleared. Kurt helped me sit up. The pain in my right shoulder was intense.

The farm was owned by a Swiss woman who had seen my fall. She ran across the pasture screaming again and again, "You have broken your clavacola! You have broken your clavacola!"

Soon I was propped up in the back seat of her old car. She drove as if demons were after us, racing along every bumpy shortcut on her way to the hospital. I hurt too much to complain, and besides I knew it wouldn't slow her down.

After the doctor took X rays of my shoulder and neck, he confirmed my injury as a separated shoulder that would require surgery. He applied a proper sling, and ordered a generous shot of narcotic which the nurse jabbed into my hip. I decided that I would rather have surgery in the hospital where I worked in Seattle, and the doctor allowed that, although sore, I was fit to travel. It was about an hour's drive to my home. He handed me an envelope of narcotic pills for later.

After we got back to the farm, Kurt and I loaded our truck and I decided he should drive as much as possible. I would take over when we came to a town or congested area. He had only driven on back roads before that day, but he did drive us home — at twenty-five miles per hour, ignoring the obscene gestures of drivers who roared past us, honking and swearing.

The next day I was wheeled into surgery. I joked with the anesthesiologist who threatened to shave off half of my full beard. He said, "Sleep well" and infused the anesthetic. My first recollection after surgery was waking up in my room three different times that first night. Each time there was a different Marlon Brando movie on television. First Napoleon, then a cowboy, and finally the punchy fighter in *On the Waterfront.* I couldn't get myself oriented because the nurses were so attendant. Every time I woke up and seemed in pain, they gave me another shot of morphine.

By morning, I was in urinary retention, a condition I no longer treat as casually in others as I did before I experienced it myself. My lower abdomen felt as though it would explode. It was one of those times when being a college graduate is of no help. I would have signed away my house for relief. Once the catheter had emptied my bladder, I turned to breakfast. Eating was difficult for me because my right arm was trussed to my chest. While I wondered what to do, the nurses whom I worked with on the neurology ward marched in and fed me as if I were a child.

I was still afraid I wouldn't be able to urinate on my own when the time came. The thought of an indwelling catheter for a few days did not appeal to me in the least. My father phoned and I explained the problem to him. A while later he arrived with a cough-syrup bottle that held about four ounces of bourbon. He said he was prescribing "the old police remedy" for me, and if I drank half now, and half in two hours, I would have no further trouble expelling my urine. I did and I didn't.

For the next several weeks I endured many PT treatments, short for physical therapy. The therapist said in cases like mine, PT stood for pain and torture. I had gone back to work a few days after the surgery with my arm still in a sling. I wrote by holding the tablet under my right hand and moving them both as required.

Even though I avoided taking medicines during the day, by the time I arrived home in the evening, I couldn't go any longer without something to control the pain. I became more uncomfortable in my innards as the days passed. Constipation had never afflicted me before, but it did now. I tried laxatives and prunes but the task at hand was more than they could accomplish. One day, I decided to launch an all-out attack on my distended and indolent bowel. I swallowed three strong pills and inserted a charge at the other end.

At first it sounded like thunder accompanied by rumbles and squeals I'd never heard before. I braced myself on the stool, and wished I were wearing a helmet in case I hit the ceiling. No ordinary toilet could handle such a volume, and despite repeated flushings it soon plugged up and overflowed. When it was over, I felt like a deflated dirigible.

This was the first time I came to appreciate how much more enjoyable it is to be a doctor than a patient, and that the high from Percodan never changes anything.

II

One July Saturday I decided to trim back the willows that grew along the edge of the bank in front of my cabin on Marrowstone Island. It was the day before our annual picnic for the staff teaching at the Centrum Writer's Workshop in Port Townsend. The willows were blocking part of the view of the water. Because I was an ardent chain-saw user I decided to fire up my twenty-inch Stihl and mow them down.

I also had my first bifocals and kept reminding myself to keep my head tilted down so that I could see through the top half of the glasses and keep my eye on my work. I sat on the bank with my legs out in front of my body and held the whining saw at arm's length and sideways as I slaughtered the willows. The saw was heavy and my arms tired. As I leaned backward and lifted the saw across my legs, I didn't clear the right one. I felt a heavy thump against my right shin and looked down at a greasy and bloody tract through my pants and flesh.

I shut the saw off and pressed by handkerchief against the wound. If I bled to death, it would be my own fault. After hobbling into the cabin I searched for bandages. The pain was now excruciating, and I had trouble keeping pressure on the wound as I rummaged through the drawers in the bathroom.

The phone rang. A friend who lived at Mystery Bay, two miles up the road from my place, happened to call me about oysters. He said I didn't sound well. When he heard about my injury he told me to stay put, and within minutes he was driving me into a medical clinic in Port Townsend.

The family doctor on call was an old friend, and he spent nearly two hours cleaning the wound and sewing the tissues together in the proper order. I knew that as a neurologist who never touched these kinds of emergencies I couldn't have done the same for him. I also learned what it was to utterly depend upon someone, and how patients must feel toward me when I care for them during injuries and illnesses. He comforted me when he said he'd repaired lots of chain-saw injuries, and he proved it by the way he treated mine.

The local anesthetic left me feeling pretty good for the rest of the day. When my wife and family arrived that evening I calmly explained what had happened. By the next morning my leg was so swollen and painful that I had to keep it elevated. The pain required narcotics to keep it under reasonable control. The Centrum faculty included as visiting writers Robert Bly, John Haines and Denise Levertov. I remember Denise preparing a plate of food and serving me in my chair.

My wife drove us home the following morning and I spent the next two weeks with my foot elevated on the back of the couch where I lay in our living room. My fever persisted several days and I developed a right footdrop. During my recovery, I most enjoyed the nights, when I could settle down undisturbed and read. Poet Philip Levine had once said that reading *War and Peace* by Tolstoy was a turning point in his life. I knew of a hardback copy resting on a shelf of a church library, and I arranged to have it delivered. The characters in that novel became part of my life and I read by the hour, dozing off for a time, then resuming the story. I wondered if all national leaders shouldn't take enough time away from their duties to read about the futility of mankind seeking military solutions to their differences as nations and peoples. It was worth the injury to me to have so much time with Tolstoy.

I still have a bit of a limp, and the top of my right foot and part of my shin goes numb when I am tired or the weather turns cold. These things remind me how carelessness led me into the hands of an excellent doctor, and temporary invalidism led me to *War and Peace*. I benefited mightily from them both.

III

On a misty New Year's Eve afternoon I stood at the top of the stairs that led to my beach at Marrowstone Island. The tide was receding, and as I looked down I could see where clam poachers had been digging in recent days. They were in a hurry and didn't bother to fill in the holes they made. I was furious.

The stairs are wooden and the staircase over thirty feet long. The persistent dampness covers wooden objects such as these stairs with a slime that is dangerously slippery for the unwary. Without thinking, I started down the stairs to get a closer look at the work of the poachers.

My feet went straight out from under me, I fell hard on my right hip and bounced down the stairs feet first. I grabbed at the only rail with my left hand, dislocating my thumb, but I managed to grab hold hard enough to stop my fall. By then I was about halfway down the stairs.

The pain in my right hip nearly paralyzed me when I tried to move. I thought it was probably fractured, and there was an enlarging swelling over the point of maximum impact. One can lose a lot of blood with a fractured hip, and I knew that was what the swelling represented. I grew weaker. I was going into shock with my head uphill, the worst possible position for me to be in. I fingered my pulse, which was slow and faint. The stairs were not wide enough for me to turn even into a horizontal position. I dared not let go with my left hand for fear I would slide farther. I was alone. No one expected me home for at least two or three more hours and it was getting dark. I could not control what would happen to me.

Within minutes terrible pain in my right hip and left thumb subsided as I drifted into the most peaceful reverie I have ever experienced. The air was quiet. My dog sat near me giving what comfort she could but unable to provide real help. I could no longer keep my eyes open, and I relaxed my grip and allowed my heavy lids to drop.

Instead of the usual dark tunnel, nausea and fading characteristic of the fainting spells which I suffered from as a tall skinny boy who stood in one place too long when it was hot, I saw a brightness. I felt myself outside of my body, and I realized that my body and I were not the same thing. All pain, all fear, all guilt disappeared within the brilliant solitude where I now was. I thought if this is death, it is so peaceful, so free of suffering, and if I died at my beloved

Marrowstone it would not be so bad.

I did not see loved ones as others have reported in near-death experiences, but then I'm not sure that is what this experience was for me. But the glorious brightness was different from anything I had ever seen before, and my sense of being at one with all there was within and around me bathed me like warm soothing water.

How much time passed, I do not know. Gradually I returned into my body and my eyes opened in the dense winter twilight. The tide had moved farther out. My dog licked at my face. The heavy pain returned in my right hip, and I palpated the large swelling with my right hand. Next I grabbed hold of my left thumb with my right hand and jerked it back into place, which felt much better.

There were about fifteen stairs I had to work my way up in order to be free of danger. I managed to get on my knees, and facing up the stairs and with the greatest of care I made it to the top landing. Next was the problem of standing up, which was not as difficult as I had thought it would be. I used a piece of driftwood for a cane and hobbled into the cabin where I lay down.

It was dark as I debated whether to drive myself home or call for help. After I hobbled around a bit more, I decided that despite the collection of a pint or two of blood in my hip muscles, the bone was most likely not fractured and I could be home and in bed long before someone could fetch and drive me there. So I drove on home.

The hematoma took several weeks to resolve, and the point of the hip was tender for months. Otherwise, my recovery was uneventful. But what of those moments when I was not in my body, or experiencing that pain? It was a healing which I had never known before, the facing of something like death and finding it not so frightening. In fact it was the opposite. Everything about that place and time was so natural, so blissful, a spiritual excursion into lands we seldom have the chance to travel.

PART THREE

Life Support

The Bookstore

A MONDAY morning in my office. My schedule is modest and I encounter no serious illnesses nor demanding diagnostic problems among the first patients of the day. As all physicians know, one requirement of our profession is that we take appropriate and personal interest in whatever the patient brings us. For a neurologist it is often the vagaries of chronic neck or low back pain, an unexplainable tingling, a dizziness the patient has trouble describing clearly but fears may be multiple sclerosis, and our rent-payer, headaches. I suspect headache patients are to the neurologist what menstrual-cramps patients are to the gynecologist, constipation patients are to the gastroenterologist and post-micturition dribbling patients are to the urologist.

The case histories in each of these conditions are familiar to us who spend much of our time listening to patients. I often settle back in my chair searching for something the patient says to capture my interest. When nothing such is present I remind myself to think of a means by which I may be helpful to this person. I know of too many cases where the neurotic or hysteric was later found to have a brain tumor, the early stages of a vasculitis, or something equally serious. No patient has a more righteous fury than one who has been dismissed by a physician as having nothing of consequence wrong with their health only to have another physician discover the truth: it is as they feared and they are indeed ill.

When I have a cold or a headache of my own, listening demands a special effort. If I can remember that each patient is unique, my practice remains full of surprises and fascination. Headaches may be standard stuff to me but they are special to whoever has them. I am sad when I hear about physicians who have not taken time to listen to patients. And I know I'm not immune from the temptation to cut things short when I think I know the answer. Over the years it remains true that my most common mistakes are the result of not obtaining the full medical history.

Despite such philosophical admonitions and a psychological pep talk, I grow restless on this Monday as the noon hour approaches. I am tired from three hours of steady one-to-one interaction with patients. Another of the dilemmas of my practice is that while I love fascinating neurological mysteries, I am happy for the patient when I cannot come up with anything serious. Disgruntled patients who feel cheated when the results of the work-up are negative, are often taken up short when I ask them if finding cancer of the brain or a progressive and untreatable central nervous-system disorder would give them a sense of money well spent. After the shock wears off, I temper my remarks by saying that all of us like simple answers for complicated problems, even though we seldom find them.

A morning of patients who are not seriously ill leaves me the noon hour free and I hear a faint calling as I finish the final entry in a chart. After this many years I recognize the urge and I know it is time for me to spring into action. I will forego lunch in order to visit one of my favorite places, the

Elliott Bay Book Company on First and Main. I check my messages, nothing there that can't wait, and slip out the back door before anyone can interfere with my plans. The breeze from the bay refreshes me as I park my small pickup truck under the Alaskan Way Viaduct and walk the familiar and warped sidewalks.

As usual, the store is crowded at noon. My first stop is the table in front of the sales counter where new books of high quality are displayed. There are many excellent works for me to consider. I turn the pages of several, listening carefully, but none of them call my name. Today, any voices calling me do not come from the main table.

I move to the section across the room and on the other side of the stairwell where the books on psychology are kept. There's a voice, coming from the second shelf down, fifth book from the left. I find my first quarry, a volume entitled *The Essential Jung,* selected and introduced by a psycho-analyst, Anthony Storr, whose work I admire. This book is a welcome addition to my collection of Jung and Jungians. Storr is a careful and terse writer and I know this collection is precisely what he wants it to be. And I also know that I can never learn all the lessons contained therein. But I will try, carrying the book with me from time to time, underlining, making notes in the margins, all the while wishing I could remember more of what I read.

It is getting to be time to leave, but I have a sense that my safari is not concluded. I elbow my way through a narrow hallway and stop at another table for a brief glance at new volumes of poetry. Although there are books by familiar authors whose work I respect and some of whom I have met personally, their poems do not call me. Perhaps another time but not today. Moving on past the large racks of print collections, I take a sharp left and travel to the back shelves where the section on essays and criticism is located. Still I hear no seductive voices and I am puzzled. Only the philosophy and religion sections are left before I try fiction. My time has nearly run out and I don't know when I'll get back here.

One of the store's buyers calls me over and enthuses about a new book of essays on the poetry of Robert Bly. We are both Bly fans. He tells me the book is still boxed in the storeroom. (Perhaps that is why its cry is muffled and I cannot locate it.) Within minutes he wipes the shipping dust from a copy and hands it to me, *Robert Bly, When Sleepers Awaken,* edited by Joyce Peseroff, published by the University of Michigan Press. No doubt about it, that's a book for me. I'd recognize that voice anyplace. I scan the table of contents and read some chapter titles: "Inward to the World," "Like Those Before We Move Towards the Death We Love," "Rejoice in the Gathering Darkness," "Walking Where the Plows Have Been Turning," and "Back to the Snowy Fields." But for me it is back to the office.

The first afternoon patient is waiting as I hurry in the rear door of our small clinic, jam my coat in the closet and apologize for being a bit late. She is a middle-aged stocky woman who tells me I am twenty-seven minutes late and she thought I might have gone golfing.

Not quite, I said. I've been hunting.

She gives me an odd look, and I think she may be wishing she'd gone to the Mason Clinic instead. After I explain where I've been and show her the results of my expedition, she loses interest in her headaches and tells me about her poetry, a subject she never raises with others for fear of embarrassment. Like many who love to write, she keeps her work a secret, probably locked in a bottom desk drawer, fingerprints wiped clean from the manuscript so she can never be incriminated if it falls into the wrong hands.

Soon we are trekking the paths of her medical history. I learn more things about her that she has kept secret, and we sort out a few inner turmoils that generate her frequent and disabling migraines.

The Success of Failure

WHETHER he knew it or not, the poetry reading Richard Hugo gave in June 1975 at the Fort Worden theater was meant for me. At age forty, my old ways in life had failed me, although I preferred to blame others: wife, children, politicians or anyone else who irritated me. I took up writing as an act of unrecognized revenge, a means of setting a few things straight in the world. After all, I led a successful and exciting life in my speciality of neurology, and I felt strongly about certain issues and wanted to speak out for what I perceived to be the common good.

So between 1972 and 1974 I wrote a novel about the burden of an unjust malpractice action against a young physician, a story that dealt with the ruthlessness often displayed by lawyers toward doctors. It was a timely subject because malpractice insurance premiums were skyrocketing and there had been a physicians' strike in protest in California.

My manuscript was not received by literary agents in the same enthusiastic spirit with which I had sent it off. Their rejection letters were to the point, but I still had confidence in my message. With the right kind of help I could tidy up my work and get it published.

In June 1975 I attended the Centrum Writers' Workshop

at Fort Worden in Port Townsend, Washington on the edge of the Strait of Juan de Fuca. Fort Worden is an old ex-military base with lots of land and converted buildings that add up to a fine facility for music, art and writing conferences.

The major attraction for me was Jessamyn West, best known for her novel *The Friendly Persuasion,* but who, although in her seventies, had another best seller, *The Fall Creek Massacre,* on the charts. I felt sure she could help me, but she wouldn't be there until the second week.

The June weather was miserable even for here, and I drove the fifty miles to Fort Worden in a heavy rain. I carried with me notebooks, things I wanted to read and the manuscript of my novel. As I registered at the Centrum office, I noticed how much I looked like a writer. I had a full beard, dark brown in those days, and I wore jeans and a scruffy coat like the other men at the conference. I learned that most of the other students were poets and thus small-minded in my opinion. As for me, I was after the biggest fish of all, the best-selling novel.

Alice Walker was one of the visiting writers and I was assigned to her workshop for the first week. On the second day we had a personal conference to discuss a sample chapter of my novel, now entitled *Negligence.* (I still refuse to mention the original title in public.) She summarized what she had read in one succinct phrase: "Nothing works." Alice Walker was not long on subtlety in those days. She said I wrote like I was describing a television program. She asked how I could expect to write worthwhile fiction from such a shallow perspective that had no life, no blood, nothing that made a reader care about the characters. Being a successful neurologist might be a useful, even noble, profession, but it probably made creative writing more difficult for me because I was steeped in the prose of medical reports, which are known for their flatness and predictability. She offered little hope of my improving unless I found something I deeply cared about and wrote about people whose stories showed their own crises, tragedies and triumphs.

There was nothing I could say for there is no defending terrible writing. We spent the last few minutes of our conference talking about how bad the food was in the cafeteria. I mulled over her comments during lunch and realized that I had unwittingly picked a title that fit my fiction-writing skills.

I tried reworking my novel, but it was hopeless. So I enjoyed what I could of the workshops for the rest of the week, and kept my wounded pride out of sight and my mouth shut in Alice Walker's class.

Alice Walker left the soggy Pacific Northwest the morning following her reading at the theater. I hoped I hadn't driven her away single-handedly, although there were others in her workshop who wrote no better than I did. Writers who teach in open workshops should know that a lot of stumblers and hackers will attend, but that seemed difficult for her to accept. I understood better after her own spectacular reading. She began by announcing that she wrote in order to stay alive, and she persuaded me.

But I had no such position as hers from which to write: a black female from the South who fought for civil rights and told stories about people who were given no chance simply because they were black, female or both. I was white, middle-class, male, professional. I was what was wrong with America.

I lived at my beach cabin on Marrowstone Island during the workshop and commuted the fifteen miles to and from the classes and readings. The lush green, the ever-changing wind and sea, and the silent clouds sustained me then as they have since, when times are tough. On clear nights I could see the Point Wilson lighthouse at Fort Worden winking at me from several miles away.

There were writers at the conference more easily approachable than Alice Walker, and I met several who have remained my friends. One was James Welch, whose first novel, *Winter in the Blood,* had just put him on the front page of *The New York Times Book Review.* In an effort to soothe my bruised ego, I decided that I would host a picnic and clam feast on Sunday at my beach cabin for the faculty if they were interested. My wife, Mary, would be there for the weekend and was willing to help. The tide was low enough to insure good clamming, and the instructors would have a chance to enjoy each other without students badgering them at every turn. Jim Welch liked the idea, and soon we had most of the faculty lined up.

Jim wanted to invite his close friend and neighbor from Missoula, Richard Hugo, a famous poet coming to teach the second week of the workshop. Hugo, who had just remarried, was bringing his new wife and two stepchildren with him and Jim was sure they would all like to come to my picnic. Jim offered to introduce me to Hugo at a Centrum party the night before.

The name Richard Hugo seemed familiar, but I couldn't place it. Even though I had no interest in reading the work of the other faculty poets, I followed a strong urge to buy a book of Hugo's poems. On Saturday afternoon I tried "The Death of the Kapowsin Tavern" and several other poems without much success. I simply had no ear for what he wrote. But at least I learned a few titles I could mention in conversation if worst came to worst.

That night I wandered ill at ease among the partygoers at the old commandant's house at Fort Worden. There were real writers milling around chatting with each other and I wasn't one of them. By then I realized that even my workshop with Jessamyn West the next week wouldn't change that. My impulse to write was badly blunted and I had no idea what to do about it.

Several people were gathered around a large table in the kitchen where they regaled each other with tales that brought laughter. (I was thankful Alice Walker wasn't there describing my novel to them.) Their appearance was somewhere between casual and shaggy. Most of the men wore beards and beads while the women wore long straight hair and cotton shirts too large for them. I spied one man whose ethereal countenance suggested great sensitivity. Could that be Hugo?

Jim Welch elbowed his way through the crowd, tapped me on the shoulder and pointed out a heavy man who sat with his back to me. I moved a bit to my left in order to see his face. He was nearly bald, clean-shaven with long sideburns, and he wore the short jacket of a truck driver. He inhaled deeply on a cigarette and gulped coffee between drags. His round and deeply-lined face with its heavy jowls alternated between fierce scowls and wild merriment. His whiskey voice erupted into thundering laughter and he looked like a favorite uncle at a family picnic.

Jim grinned. "That's him."

Hugo stood up to be introduced, squeezed my hand in a powerful grip and beamed with enthusiasm as I described the proposed picnic. He called over his new wife, Ripley, introduced us and asked if they could bring anything. His friendliness was disarming, without pretension.

Dick Hugo and I hit it off right from the start. We spent much of the time at the picnic in conversation. It turned out that we had grown up not far from each other in West Seattle, I on Elmgrove Street, he in White Center. He was about ten years older than me and we had not known each other when we were kids. But we knew the same streets, schools, playgrounds, movie theaters, and we were both avid baseball players. During World War Two, he was a bombardier in the real Air Force, while I slaughtered legions of the enemy with my plywood gun in the woods surrounding my house.

Dick treated his life as a poet as a lot less interesting than mine as a neurologist. We were soon on the subject of his health and my adventures as a doctor. We physicians learn that we usually spend a certain amount of social conversation discussing medicine. Maybe it makes up for the high fees people pay when they see us professionally. Dick and I had both attended the University of Washington and we relived the football teams of our days and our experiences with professors we had in common. There seemed no end to what we could think of to say to each other.

Suddenly I placed the name Hugo. I had taken care of his first wife when I was a resident in neurology at the University Hospital in Seattle and my professor was her attending physician. She suffered from a cervical root syndrome, the medical term for a pinched nerve in her neck. They were divorced several years later.

He was hard to beat as a storyteller and was in turn a most appreciative audience. Much of what we laughed at wasn't funny in hindsight and our language was crude, which added to our fun. We were two kids happily playing in the mud.

Monday we ate lunch together in the cafeteria at Fort

Worden. He asked me if I was coming to his workshop. I could think of no graceful way to decline his invitation. Besides, I was curious as to what kind of teacher he was. Soon we walked across the large mowed field to the repainted old schoolhouse where he would meet his class. Once inside the small classroom, he settled himself at the head of the table in what I came to recognize as typical Hugo fashion. He set out a battered folder of papers, a package of cigarettes, an ashtray, a cigarette lighter, a thermos of coffee and a couple of candy bars.

It was incongruous to me that this lumbering, good-natured fat man with the earthy sense of humor was a poet, let alone an English teacher. He was blue-collar to the core and proud of it, a liver-and-onions man, a Pendleton shirt man, an avid fisherman and a steady drinker in bars until forced to quit a couple of years earlier after he nearly bled to death from a duodenal ulcer.

First off he recited a poem, "The Rattlesnake," by Brewster Ghiselin:

> I found him sleepy in the heat
> And dust of a gopher burrow,
> Coiled in loose folds upon silence
> In a pit of the noonday hillside.
> I saw the wedged bulge
> Of the head hard as a fist.
> I remembered his delicate ways:
> The mouth of a cat's mouth yawning.
> I crushed him deep in dust,
> And heard the loud seethe of life
> In the dead beads of the tail
> Fade, as wind fades
> From the wild grain of the hill.

He repeated it several times emphasizing how its images, metaphors and rhythms made it a fine poem. I was moved, but I wasn't sure if it was by the poem or his dramatic reading. Either way, I hadn't heard language that beautiful for as long as I could remember.

Next he went up to the blackboard and wrote out a few lines of one of his poems.

> With the Stilli this defeated and the sea
> turned slough by close Camano, how can water die
> with drama, in a final rich cascade,
> a suicide, a victim of terrain, a martyr?

He pointed out the sounds that echoed from line to line and told how he picked words that seemed unrelated but sounded similar enough to stimulate associations that otherwise might never occur to the reader or listener.

He discussed language, what one could do with it, what makes a fine poem, and how good writing lives a life of its own. I felt myself come alive, as if there was hope for me in some way not yet clear. Students passed out copies of the poems they wished to present and read them aloud to the class. Utter silence followed while Dick spent several moments deep in thought as he studied the poem in front of him, puffing on his cigarette and drinking coffee. He looked up, asked for discussion, then offered his own comments about the poem. Here was a psychoanalyst in action, pointing out where the poet lost heart or tried to avoid saying what the speaker in the poem wanted to say because it was too hard. A visiting poet who sat in on one session told me it was like a masters' class with Beethoven.

I was hooked deep in the gullet and I attended all of Dick's workshops that week. We continued to spend off-time together, Dick with his constant coffee and cigarettes, me nursing a beer or soft drink, but afraid I would get sick if I smoked that much. I feared I was becoming a pest.

In my enthusiasm I wrote what I thought were poems and showed them to Dick. He scowled, puffed on his cigarette and thought of what he could say and spare my feelings. He suggested that I read Roethke, Yeats and some other lyric poets to help develop my ear. He sensed my seriousness about writing and encouraged me to work hard at it. He told me that everyone starts at the beginning, and even after many years of teaching he couldn't tell who would become a good writer and who wouldn't.

I also attended Jessamyn West's workshop. But I knew there was little point in showing her my novel, and so I learned what I could from the writing of others and enjoyed her discussions of short stories. Delightful though she was, my heart was with Hugo.

Dick gave his poetry reading the last night of the conference and the theater was packed with friends, colleagues, students and other admirers. He was in fine form, reciting most of his poems, as was his habit. His poems were about hard times, defeats, abandoned places, forgotten names, being degraded, and somehow finding hope and courage, even successes which were often unexpected.

Lines from "The Freaks at Spurgeon Road Field" tore me open.

> The dim boy claps because the others clap.
> The polite word handicapped is muttered in the stands.
> Isn't it wrong the way the mind moves back?

Farther on in the same poem:

The score is always close, the rally always short.
I've left more wreckage than a quake.

Another line:

The afflicted never cheer in unison.

After the first few poems, he apologized because his poetry was so sad. He wanted to assure everyone how much fun he was in real life. We all roared.

From a Port Townsend poem:

A novel fakes a start in every bar.

And from "What Thou Lovest Well Remains American":

You remember the name was Jensen. She seemed old
always alone inside, face pasted gray to the window,
and mail never came.

Between poems he described how he elected to try for charm rather than courage after the terror he experienced flying in combat over Europe. He said he was stationed in Italy and had a lot of trouble regarding the Italians as enemies because they were so friendly.

And so the reading went, this jovial fat man now a creative-writing teacher in Montana, who grew up in White Center, survived a bomber crash in World War Two, studied poetry with Theodore Roethke at the University of Washington, worked in an office at Boeing for thirteen years because it was safe (he published poems regularly during those years), eventually giving up the safe life to return to the places in Italy where he was stationed during the war. From that trip came new poems and his job at the University of Montana.

He described his mistakes, his sense of failure and how hard it was to go on when he was lonely and discouraged. But he did go on because his life was all he had. He said that none of us are as good as we think, nor are we better than those we degrade. Inside, we are all much more alike than we care to admit. And through it all there was the language, the gorgeous music of his metaphors, images, slant rhymes, all the wonder of his poetic craftsmanship, underpinned by a ruthless honesty about life as he saw it.

I drove home that night playing the tape of his reading that I had made, happy that I was alive and that it was not too late to learn to write. Richard Hugo had showed me how one can come to terms with one's life through writing, and if he, being the outrageous person he was, could succeed, then there was hope for the likes of me.

During the ensuing winter, I listened many times to that tape, read and reread his poems, as well as the poems of Roethke, Stafford, Yeats, and the work of many others including James Welch and Alice Walker. I tried a few poems in a local workshop, and wrote in my journal. And I came to know that I would have to write no matter what, and that there were things I cared passionately about, even if I had to search painfully within myself to find them.

Although complaining about the weather is standard Puget Sound conversation, both Dick Hugo and I loved the Pacific Northwest. Unexpected fog and mist on any morning, rain on the Fourth of July parade, constantly resculptured clouds, countless saltwater bays with enlarging and diminishing beaches, whitecaps charging under a furious southwest storm, winter snow blazing on the sunlit Olympics, slow summer twilights, days in winter that are never-changing gray, evergreens unchanged no matter what the day or weather — these are what we pilgrims of this region find breathing in our bones. This territory and this weather tugs at me with the sense of always returning home, not to a house but to some old neighborhood where I have always lived and where I am from. We are seldom the stable, self-controlled, civilized, evolutionarily improved species we like to think we are. Our terrain, tides and the always unpredictable weather teach us that. So does Richard Hugo's poetry. So does the daily living of our lives.

One overcast July morning the Hugos' old convertible rolled into the driveway of our home on Bainbridge Island. Dick pulled himself from the car, his usual limp, which he attributed to a childhood injury, apparent. (Some of his more romantic admirers hoped the bad hip was from a war wound.) His constant frowns and squints turned into a broad smile and wave when he spotted me in the garden.

Ripley, quiet and graceful but equally friendly, seemed to enjoy watching these two refugees from West Seattle reunited. She told me Dick had been busy with poetry workshops, readings and his own writing for several months. They were both ready for a rest and some time together.

Marrowstone Island is just what the doctor ordered, said Dick.

My wife was out on an errand. I made coffee for the three of us. Dick sat down at the large oak table, set out his cigarettes, summoned an ashtray, lit a Benson and Hedges and surveyed the spacious country kitchen of our sixty-year-old farmhouse. He liked sitting at tables. A table is where friends enjoy conversations, a place to rest on one's elbows, set down a coffee cup or a whiskey glass, assemble the paraphernalia of smoking. And it is where he wrote.

We picked up right where we had left off the previous summer with that ease that marks friendship. Time is irrelevant in friendship, and whether friends meet after days, months or years makes little difference. The continuity is still there.

Three days later, on a bright gull-soaring day, Mary, Ripley, Dick, and I toured Marrowstone Island. We talked with two boys as they fished from a tilted abandoned dock. They weren't upset because they weren't catching fish. They were fishing. Dick recalled fishing as a boy from the Fauntleroy ferry dock in West Seattle for shiners and flounders. I'd fished there too. We both admitted we'd never caught much, but we had faithfully attended to the business of fishing.

One time when I was ten or eleven, I fished from that dock while my mother patiently waited for me. A rough shipyard worker shoved me aside with his boot as he walked toward the ferryboat. My mother protested, and he was foul-mouthed to her. We were both humiliated. That night I told my father, who was a police detective. He said he would "have a little talk with him." My father grew up with no father of his own and knew what it was like to be bullied. He had his own sense of justice when it came to matters involving his wife and children.

The three of us went to the ferry dock the next day. My mother and I pointed out the man, and my father made me go with him as he called the man over. I was scared because my father was overmatched in both size and weight. He flashed his badge and asked for the burly man's identification. Then in a quiet voice and clear language he explained to the astonished shipyard worker the stark consequences of hassling children. The man apologized. My father told us, as we drove home, "He's not a bad guy. He just needed a little talking to."

Dick loved the story. He'd been raised by his grandparents, with no father to protect him. The four of us stopped to wander through Sound View Cemetery, which overlooks Admiralty Inlet from a high bluff. Our reason for stopping was, according to Dick, because no one else would unless they had loved ones buried there. The gravestones were old and simple, with the names nearly ground off by winter weather. Deer grazed near us. We talked about the dead: fishermen, mothers who died in childbirth, disillusioned immigrants who found the American dream a nightmare and failed here as they had in the old country, farmers who relished the peaceful island life, children whose view of the world was the quiet life of deer and cattle, and those who came back from some distant city to be buried and left alone. I remember one gravestone with the name worn on the stone, and below the name, "Airman First Class." No celebrities, statesmen or other famous people.

One evening we had a supper at home on Bainbridge with the Hugos as special guests and a few friends who were good company. All of us but Dick drank wine. Dick was then on the wagon, and he stuck with coffee. Following the meal and still sitting at the table, of course, Dick recited two or three poems, including one based on the story of an Indian fugitive in Montana who hid in the mountains with his wife. One day he heard someone coming, hid behind the door and swung an axe at the intruder. It was not the police, it was his wife, and he had killed her by tragic accident.

One guest was a woman who is shy and often ill at ease with strangers. She caught Dick's attention. He asked her if she felt ill, for he had noticed she seemed uncomfortable and he worried about her. She smiled and replied she felt fine. He asked if she was sure. She broke into laughter and from then on joined in.

It reminded me of the time Dick and I were walking across a large field to the schoolhouse at Fort Worden where he held his workshop each afternoon. Suddenly he spotted a woman from his class walking ahead of us. He said that he owed her an apology because he was unkind about her poem the day before and had embarrassed her. He hailed her while I moved out of earshot. Soon I heard his mighty laugh and saw that her face was broad with joy. Later Dick said to me that he should know better than to criticize such a person in front of others.

The Hugos went on their way. The glory of Indian summer yielded to a rainy fall, which in turn gave way to a pesky, soaking winter with eight to nine hours per day of lead-colored daylight.

I labored with my own writing, trying some poetry, thinking about starting another novel and often recalling the Hugo line, "A novel fakes a start in every bar." Richard Hugo sounds and rhythms burned in my brain, and I imagined myself writing about loneliness, despair and failure, the typical Hugo themes. I knew the feelings, but I had no language that would live in those circumstances.

The annual Theodore Roethke Poetry Reading at the University of Washington was held the day after my birthday in May 1977. The visiting poet was Dick. I regarded the event as a special present for me and was among the large crowd wedged into Roethke Auditorium that evening. I held my tape recorder on my lap and didn't ask for permission to make a recording for fear there was a rule against it.

Dick wore a suit and tie in honor of the occasion, and although he was recovering from a cold and was still hoarse, he sipped water and went ahead. As was his habit, he punctuated his hard-hitting poems with anecdotes. He told how, when he stopped drinking, he learned two important things: first, not everyone in the world is drunk; and second, not all women in the world are overwhelmingly beautiful. After he sobered up, he said, he found he had so much more time to do things. He wrote with his old enthusiasm, marveling at the words and phrases that came forth on the page. His lifelong love affair with baseball led him to try right field one night for a short-handed team, and he even punched a hit over the second baseman's head.

He said that when he began teaching at the University of Montana there were several among the small English faculty who hated him for being a poet, and when he worked at Boeing there were sixty-three thousand employees and none of them hated him for being a poet.

A young couple, students most likely, sat on the stairs next to my aisle seat. He carried the leather shoulder bag of a writer. He was dressed in jeans, sandals and a tattered shirt with its frayed collar partially covered by his long dark hair and beard. His attractive companion, slender and full in the best places, sat motionless in rapt attention. Several times he muttered to her in disbelief, his eyes moist from being touched somewhere deep inside by this man who made no scholarly pretenses about the life we all lead if we are honest with ourselves. I knew this feeling well.

After the reading, I waited in a long line to shake hands

and renew our friendship. In the last year he had come to Seattle every few months and never called me, not out of discourtesy or neglect, I assumed, but because he had other friends here who went back many years. I worried that he might not recognize me. After all, I had more reason to remember him than he had to remember me. He had done more for my life than I had for his.

He dissolved my worries with a prompt "Hi, Bob." His memory for names of people and everything else was enviable. He believed that poets should pay attention to details. We had only a moment, but without hesitation he invited Mary and me to visit him and Ripley on the island of Skye, in Scotland. He was soon leaving on a Guggenheim fellowship for a year.

By the time I wrote to the Hugos in Scotland of our plans to visit in the spring of 1978, they had decided to return before we could get there. I wondered if he had been insincere in his offer, and worried that I had offended him in some fashion I didn't realize. Perhaps he resented my passing myself off as a writer of sorts, or perhaps he didn't really value my friendship as much as I hoped. As one who doesn't make lasting friends easily, I felt defeated.

I wrote to him a time or two after he returned to Montana but he didn't answer. His spirit continued to influence me, and I was writing essays for the local medical society magazine each month as part of my duties as editor. I had an audience to practice my writing on, and nothing helps a writer improve more than that.

One day, perhaps after a dream in which Dick appeared, I realized what was happening. Dick was drinking again. No one had to tell me. For whatever reasons, he was unable to sustain his abstinence, and I knew from others that when

Dick Hugo drank, he drank self-destructively, almost as a form of suicide. Adding drinking to his chain smoking and obesity could hardly improve his health. Thus he faced the consequences associated with all three: an intellectual decline and an over-all decrease in his abilities and energy.

I have no way of knowing whether or not any thoughts and dreams involving me were ever a part of his life. But for the next few months he was in my thoughts and dreams, just as he is today. I lost contact with him. He didn't answer letters. I phoned a time or two, but he said little and seemed anxious to hang up.

In the fall of 1979, I was invited to be a guest speaker for a creative-writing class at one of the Seattle community colleges. My monthly essays were a modest success among my medical colleagues and their families. It was the wife of one of those colleagues who invited me to speak to her classes.

By then I had a limp of my own. I was recovering from a chain-saw slash across my right shin. It was entirely my own fault, my first experience with bifocals as I had sat on the edge of a bank and cut back willows. I simply didn't clear my right shin when I lifted the saw away. As a result I spent much of the summer lying on the couch with my right foot elevated, waiting for the swelling and infection to subside.

By the time I was due to speak, my right foot was still partially paralyzed and flopped as I searched unfamiliar hallways for the assigned classroom. I passed a suite of faculty offices and noticed a poster announcing a poetry reading by Richard Hugo in three weeks. Hugo and I talking about creative writing in the same college. Incongruous, except that he got paid a lot more than I did. For me it was an honor, for him it was his work. Nothing could keep me from attending his reading.

The October morning was a football day, leaves making their longest possible glides in the chilly breeze, while acrobatic clouds performed in the bright sun. I walked from my car toward the auditorium where Dick would read. A small car eased towards me, its left front window rolled down, revealing a familiar scowling face with lips pressed tight on a cigarette, peering at the buildings, no doubt searching for the right one. I waved. Dick looked at me, blank for a moment, then honked the horn as he pulled into a parking slot. He struggled out of the car and limped toward me and I started to remind him of who I was. He was offended, scolding me for thinking he would not recognize me. He apologized for not answering my letters. He'd been so busy with his teaching and writing that he had to let a lot of things go.

As we walked he said he was disappointed when I didn't show up at his reading at the University of Washington earlier that week, and he hoped it wasn't because I was mad at him.

He was very heavy, his face puffy and swollen, his general color poor. He coughed when he pulled at his cigarette and spat gobs of heavy phlegm. His hands shook, and his voice was raspy and he labored with his breathing. He said this was his ninth poetry reading in ten days and he was tired. It was hard on him to give poetry readings and drink too, he said with a mirthless laugh.

He wore a Pendleton shirt open at the neck, a tweed sportcoat and nondescript slacks. The head of the English department introduced Dick in flowery and humorous terms, and Dick roared with laughter at all the right times. Dick gave a brief talk on teaching creative writing and said that when he started he gave everyone A's because he didn't want to hurt anyone's feelings. The school administration called him to task so he grew tougher, although he still felt guilty when someone failed his class. It meant he hadn't done his job as a teacher. He then talked about how hard it was to decide how good a writer would be. Some of the most extravagantly dressed social rebels had quite ordinary minds, while a young woman who quietly raised her two children might have a rich interior life upon which to draw. He talked about ordinary-appearing people who are extraordinary, such as poet William Stafford.

We chatted during the intermission and took up right where we had left off two years before. But despite his exuberance, some of the spark was missing. Whether he realized that or not I don't know, but I did know it was pointless to talk with him about his health in the brief time we had. I invited him and Ripley to visit us at Marrowstone the next summer.

He gave his poetry reading while seated on a stool behind a lectern, with his books and papers arranged in front of him. He announced to the audience that he was coming to Marrowstone Island the next summer to visit me, and if someone wanted to arrange a workshop for him to teach the week before and collect the money, he would do so. But, no matter what, he would be at Marrowstone where he could watch the tide come home at night.

The workshop was arranged and held as scheduled but I didn't attend, to my everlasting regret. Later, when I asked him how it went, he said the participants were much better critics than poets.

Dick and Ripley pulled into our Marrowstone place on a perfect summer day, with clouds high and white, gentle breezes from the mirrored bay, maple and alder trees the richest green, great blue herons feeding at a minus-three-foot tide, clams spurting everywhere. Mary and I had been there several days and were in the full swing of doing nothing of importance.

Dick looked hungover, heavier than ever, but he seemed happy and greeted Mary and our children by name.

I purposely didn't have any beer or whiskey in view, but before long he allowed as how a drink would hit the spot. A second and a third followed. He sat at the picnic table on the deck, languishing in the warm sun, smoking heavily, coughing and laughing. We traded stories, relived our youth in West Seattle and spent the first of several enjoyable days.

He often volunteered to help with the chores, but he never meant it, and we never took him up on it. He preferred to be served and feigned surprise when we brought him things. But we didn't mind. He knew how to get the most out of friendliness. He was particularly fond of ice cream and late-night sandwiches washed down with beer.

The Centrum poetry workshop was in its second and final week at Fort Worden, and Ripley, Mary, Dick and I went to a party every night after attending the faculty reading. The more Dick drank, the happier he became, sitting at a table, joking with the crowd gathered around him and threatening to stay indefinitely. Ripley urged me to drag him away before he became entrenched beyond all reason. And I did.

Poet Galway Kinnell was a featured teacher at the workshop. He and Dick were old friends and admirers. Galway implored Dick to take care of himself. His words fell on the ears of one who likes things as they are, no matter what the price may be tomorrow. Dick the Friendly promised to think about it and acknowledged Galway was right. The parties went on.

La Push is at the mouth of the Quillayute River on the west coast of Washington and the salmon were running, according to the man at the resort with whom I talked on the phone. I made reservations for Dick, Ripley, my daughter Colleen and myself on a charter boat for a morning's fishing.

We drove to La Push, about a hundred miles from Marrowstone, the night before and hit fog and rain at the coast. Dick said it was a good night for a murder. In the cafe at Harley's Resort, as the weather mounted its fury, Dick recited his poem "La Push" for us during our dinner of hamburgers, French fries and milkshakes.

That night we stayed in motel rooms behind Harley's resort. Dick and I slept in one room and Colleen and Ripley slept across the hall. I should say that he slept and I tried to ignore his plaster-cracking snores.

The next morning the weather had calmed and the fishing was excellent. Our charter-boat skipper was a master fisherman, and we caught two salmon apiece with no difficulty. We could have caught many more except for the limits imposed by the government and enforced by our skipper. Dick was thrilled when Ripley reeled in the first one. We celebrated as the *Susan Lee* battered through the troughs on our way in. We saw porpoises and whales, and Colleen was sure she saw shark fins. She was fourteen. After the long drive home we napped, and that night we barbequed as much fresh salmon as we could eat.

The next afternoon, Dick engaged Todd, age ten, and his friend in a poker game. The boys were wild with excitement, which moderated somewhat when they realized Dick would not give them their money back. Dick told them it was important to learn the value of money.

Ripley was worried about Dick. She said he had been in

Arkansas teaching the year before, and they made a long trip by car during which he gave many poetry readings on their way back to Montana. Dick had barely made it. Once he resumed teaching in Missoula, he arranged his schedule so that he had long weekends, and he drank considerably. His writing production was down to almost nothing. He was profoundly upset that he hadn't won the Pulitzer Prize. He blamed it on living in Montana.

When Dick and Ripley left, I had Dick's promise that he would see his doctor as soon as they returned to Missoula. I heard nothing from him until a phone call in January 1981. Meanwhile I devoured his poems and listened over and over to the three tapes I had made of him talking and reading. It was as if he had helped me find an earthy side of myself that I had kept hidden in the shadows of my soul.

One January morning I picked up my office phone to hear that wonderful gruff voice filled with worry. Dick had a shadow on his chest X ray that wouldn't clear. His doctors didn't know what it was and he was coming to the Virginia Mason Hospital in Seattle for further tests. He worried it was cancer and so did I. I kidded him about not coming to Swedish Hospital where I did most of my inpatient work, but it was a bad joke. His doctor in Missoula preferred Mason, and Dick preferred I be his friend and not his doctor. I was thankful for that. Mary and I would visit him our first chance. I asked if he liked flowers. He said he preferred hamburgers.

Our first visit was on a Sunday, shortly after he checked in, and I had a bag full of hamburgers for our lunch. Dick was deeply worried and all efforts at good humor failed. The night before, one of his doctors told Dick that his smoking days were over, gathered up his cigarettes, tore them in pieces and threw them into the wastebasket. Dick was startled and demanded to know why. The doctor replied, "High card wins." Dick was impressed and said to me, these guys don't mess around.

He had a constant parade of visitors, some of them unwelcome, but he seemed to want me there. The night before his thoracotomy, the hospital chaplain came by to pray for him. Dick told the chaplain he'd been lucky before. If he'd survived a plane crash, he must be destined for a long life. No one would speculate about the nature of his chest lesion before the surgery, a wise precaution, for there is no substitute for a biopsy.

Dick's only novel, a detective story entitled *Death and the Good Life*, had just been published. The main character was a cop named Al "Mush-heart" Barnes who had been ineffective on the Seattle Police Force because he was too soft-hearted and had moved to a small Montana town where he became the sheriff. Dick had used an idea of mine about overly seductive women usually being hysterical, and I was flattered. We had a hard time being jovial, even over the expected success of the book.

Dick underwent the removal of his entire right lung after the biopsy revealed adenocarcinoma, a deadly form of lung cancer which can be treated only by excision. That afternoon I tried to comfort him in the Intensive Care Unit, where he fought for air and moaned constantly with pain. He asked me if he had cancer and I said I didn't know, which was true at the time. He nodded that he thought he did, otherwise they wouldn't have taken the lung.

He barely survived the operation, and during his recovery a photographer from *Life* magazine took a photo of him standing by his bed, disheveled and only partially dressed, which they published as part of an article on major contemporary American poets. Ironically, Galway Kinnell was in the same article, and he was photographed swimming underwater in Hawaii. The contrast between the two friends was as stark as the world Richard Hugo wrote about.

Following a difficult recovery period, Dick went back to Missoula with Ripley, and after several months he resumed teaching at the university. He never smoked again, swam regularly and reluctantly dieted away many pounds, which helped his breathing to no small extent. After all, a fat man who smokes, drinks and eats excessively has three major pleasures. When he is advised to give up all three, he wonders why he gets out of bed in the morning. Dick settled for giving up two of the three. He still drank.

In the summer of 1981 we accepted the Hugos' long-standing invitation to visit them in Missoula. I wasn't sure how much he wanted me to come, but I knew Ripley did, and I wanted to see Dick alive at least once more. Mary, Todd, Colleen and I took a borrowed motor home and stopped for three days in Missoula on our way to Yellowstone National Park.

We arrived about ten o'clock one evening. Dick and I talked as usual about the wonderful West Seattle days, drinking beer in the heat, seated at the dining-room table. Amazingly, he had shown no recurrence of cancer. He said he had told me he was lucky. But he was often short of breath, and although he tried to write some poems, he had completed and published only a few, including one in memory of his good friend poet James Wright, who had died a year or so earlier of cancer. Dick said he had given a few of what he called his "one-lunged poetry readings," but it was difficult.

Even his enthusiasm for fishing had flagged, and he confided to me that he didn't expect to live a long time. He worried about Ripley, whom he loved dearly, and his two step-children, to whom he tried to be some sort of a father.

The last morning we were there we took pictures, shook hands and gave hugs all around before we turned our motor home toward Yellowstone. The last time I saw Richard Hugo he was frowning in the sun, his arm around Ripley, both of them waving goodbye.

We talked a time or two briefly on the phone, but plans for them to visit us again at Marrowstone never worked out. He kept teaching into the summer of 1982, but he did no independent workshops and wrote little.

One fall day in 1982, Dick phoned me at home. He was coming to Seattle for a poetry festival, donating his reading fee as he often did, and he was bringing his stepson Matthew along. Could I find a place for salmon fishing? Before I had completed the plans for a trip to Sekiu, he called back saying he didn't feel well. He was booked with social engagements, but shortly after his reading he went back to Missoula.

Further medical evaluation revealed he now had acute leukemia. Two malignancies in the same man. He re-entered Virginia Mason Hospital where, in the course of treatment which severely suppressed his bone marrow, he developed overwhelming sepsis and died the morning I was to visit him with a letter in my pocket with plans for another fishing trip when he was better.

The day Richard Hugo died was a Hugo day: the bluster of a gray Pacific storm, a cold biting wind, turbulent clouds pelting us with swirls of rain, whitecaps racing north on Puget Sound. It was a good day to sit at a table and write poems.

Nature's Remedy

WE do not treat silence with the proper respect. The universe, except for tiny places here and there, is empty space and silence. No noise of any kind is present as far as we know. Most of the time we find silence when we lower our heads for a moment to honor a deceased club member or colleague, or a few moments now and then when we walk alone. I propose a change.

At certain specified times, no sounds will be permitted except those essential to life, e.g., heartbeats, grass fluttering in the wind, waves washing the shore and song sparrows celebrating the sun. Talking, motors, music, machines and the cries of the tortured will cease. No matter where one is or what one does for a living, each day will contain a period of silence that will be measured by the passing of a cloud, the duration of a rainstorm or seven leaves falling from a tree.

Once we adjust to this new and different interruption, the incidence of crime and neurosis will both decline. Sleeping pills will seldom be necessary. No matter how difficult our lives, we can look forward to this time when we will not have to accomplish anything: no telephone to answer, no need to listen to anyone or anything not life-giving. All efforts to be first will be futile, for no one will cheer the winners. The center of the universe will be the center of each of us. According to the Theory of Relativity, the center of the universe can be wherever we want it to be, and I can't think of a better place for it.

We would not have to explain silence. The usual answer to what one is doing while reading is "nothing!" Given the content of much of what we read, that may be true in one sense. But reading does not equal nothing. It is even more difficult to explain why we sit alone with our fantasies, entranced by the brisk creek that runs through a mountain valley, or why we lie in bed with our hands behind our heads and the covers thrown off on a summer evening and watch the shadows play on the ceiling. It is best to claim we are planning something. Worrying about investments is respectable.

It is embarrassing to be caught meditating. Napping is more conventional and doesn't disturb our observers. Worst of all is to be caught praying, which is a sure sign of self-righteousness, big trouble or both.

Silence is not neutral. It is either the absence of tension or the building of tension. Music contains pauses. Drama requires pauses in its emotional rhythms. Silence boils forth during a power outage from a storm, or in the otherwise empty house at three o'clock on Sunday afternoon while we stare at the rain.

Silence is not necessarily loneliness. The hermit may be the least lonely of all. During silence, our ears rest and our eyes see what is not revealed by noise. Our spirits no longer sputter against their thrashing about in the waters of noise and distraction.

The writer sits at a desk with paper rolled into place in the typewriter and waits for something worth writing down to come forth. Being worthwhile limits the possibilities. Write down everything, advises the muse. Play with words, sentences, paragraphs and ideas. Waste paper. Forget lunch. This painter says she's no good. Nothing sells. All her sympathetic relatives have their walls covered with her oily canvases. Find more walls, advises the muse. Return to your work, always return to your work. The writer writes and the painter paints.

The composer ignores the ringing telephone for he hears only the internal melodies. The song is obscure and won't come out. After a while the composer jabs at the piano keys. The muse reminds the composer that it is better to swim on than to float in the calm of good intention.

The poet rearranges lines, crosses out phrases, circles words that don't fit. The point is not just to write a good poem, but to write what wants to be said. The muse prods the poet to say the unpleasant: we are not as good as we think. The muse puts down nonsense words to remind the poet who is in charge. The world will never again be as it is this moment.

The rabbi fights with his sermon. Dare he say what he knows to be true? The muse peers over his shoulder illuminating the words on the page as if they are an indictment. Silence, the voice of the muse, lifts the rabbi's soul and loosens the grip of sound on his heart. He is warm with inspiration. He will not get to the fundraiser tonight, for if he quits now, the warmth will leave and he will have another sleepless night. He sets his pen to the paper and words etch themselves in fire across the desert. He sighs. Maybe the muse doesn't like fundraisers.

The choir director snaps off the tape recording of tonight's rehearsal. The choir sounds even worse on tape. Maybe a new director is the answer. The choir at the larger church, the one with the outdated theology, can sing Bach, gospel, anything. That choir has good tenors. The director rewinds the tape and plays it again. The muse watches. There is a certain joy in those voices in spite of their poorly controlled tempos and pitches. If God's blessing depends upon close harmony, this choir hasn't a chance. But they sing in the chapel once a week. The muse smiles.

The physician studies a patient's most recent body-scan on the panel of fluorescent lights in front of him. Malignant tumors in several locations are seen as silent, inocuous-looking shadows. This is a good human being, the one with cancer, a reliable worker, loving parent, honest, a nonsmoker. This cancer should belong to a murderer who deserves this ignominious death. The physician tries for optimism in his report.

Later, while standing on the street in a fine rain, the physician turns face upward to the moon. Leaves rustle in the gutters and the pavement glistens. The muse in silence lifts the physician from somewhere deep inside. It is not too late. It is never too late until the silence is final and the moon takes full charge of the graveyards.

The Action of Grace

FLANNERY O'Connor was born in Georgia in 1925. She came from a strong Catholic family, attended parochial schools in Savannah and then Georgia State College, where she majored in social sciences. The nature of human character remained her unremitting concern and she soon decided that the answers did not lie in social sciences such as psychology. Talented as both an artist and a writer, she applied to the University of Iowa. When she got there, her Southern accent was so difficult for the Midwestern ear that she had to write out her request to Paul Engle, who ran the postgraduate writing program: "My name is Flannery O'Connor. I am not a journalist. Can I come to the Writers' Workshop?" Engle asked to see some of her work and received tough, stylish, passionate prose that would always be her hallmark. She long struggled with the concept of grace, especially its hard side, rather than love, a more common theme for fiction writers.

After her days at Iowa she moved to the artists' colony of Yaddo, at Saratoga Springs, New York, and came to know poet Robert Lowell, novelist Elizabeth Hardwick, translator and writer Robert Fitzgerald, and his wife, Sally. In 1950 while living with the Fitzgeralds in Connecticut she became seriously ill and returned home to her widowed mother, who lived alone. Dr. Arthur J. Merrill, a local internist, determined that O'Connor had systemic lupus erythematosis, and for the next nine months she was in and out of the hospital at Emory and near death more than once. Thanks to ACTH her disease finally went into remission. She was required to take either ACTH or some form of steroids from then on. She lived another fourteen years, dying in 1964 at the age of thirty-nine. The bitter irony was that her father had died of the same illness when O'Connor was fifteen, and lupus is very rare in males.

Her mother moved with O'Connor to the farm called Andalusia, five miles from Milledgeville, Georgia, where they lived for the rest of O'Connor's life. O'Connor spent those fourteen years in what for most would have been an intolerably restricted and boring existence. She and her mother maintained the farm although O'Connor could do so little of the physical work that most of it was left for the hired hands. She was chronically limited in both energy and stamina, required crutches for several years because of a painful hip, was unable to travel for more than short distances, drove an automobile only on occasion, had few neighbors other than the simple country blacks and whites who lived in an odd harmony, and raised Muscovy ducks, peafowl, Chinese geese and a variety of chickens. It did not appear a very stimulating place for a novelist and short-story writer who wanted to tell of the world and what happened to people in it.

She spent three or so hours a day on manuscripts at her typewriter and wrote countless letters to friends, editors, writers, critics, and others whom she answered only out of courtesy. If one wrote to Flannery O'Connor, one got an answer. She frequently was asked to write book reviews and criticism for various magazines and journals. She read voraciously and exchanged books by mail with many people. She never owned a television set, seldom used the telephone and avoided social events, especially cocktail parties. At times she taught at universities and colleges, but refused most invitations because of her poor health.

Her entire published output can be easily chronicled. Her three books of short stories, *The Geranium*, *A Good Man Is Hard to Find* and *Everything That Rises Must Converge* are available in a single volume entitled *Flannery O'Connor: The Complete Stories*. She authored two novels, *Wise Blood* (recently made into a movie) and *The Violent Bear It Away*, which was innocently referred to by locals by such titles as "The Valiant Bear It Always," "The Violets Bloom It Away," and her favorite, "The Bear That Ran Away with It." Sally Fitzgerald compiled and edited O'Connor's excellent essays about writing in a volume entitled *Mystery and Manners*. She also collected and arranged hundreds of O'Connor's letters into a most revealing and inspiring volume, *Habit of Being*, a title taken from the concept of Jacques Maritain that "habits are interior growths of spontaneous life," something far different from the habit of brushing one's teeth or cleaning one's plate.

She remained a Biblically oriented Catholic throughout her life and this faith gave her a special courage. She pointed out that one must suffer as much from the church as for it, and exposed follies and false piety whenever she could. Her lack of the usual whine and self-conscious complaining about the desolate, futile human condition is refreshing. Since she had no confidence in the social sciences to reveal what she wished to reveal, she protested constantly against the secularization of the Christian faith, and never indulged in self-conscious analysis of her own life nor bothered to concern herself with "coping" or "adjusting." Bitterness was not a part of her spirit.

What appears in her work is well worth considering, as are her remarkable accomplishments in spite of the misery and limitations imposed by her lupus. Throughout, her spirit remained indomitable.

A few titles of her short stories give us an idea of that spirit: "A Good Man Is Hard to Find," "The Life You Save May Be Your Own," "You Can't Be Any Poorer Than Dead," "The Enduring Chill," "Everything That Rises Must Converge," "The Lame Shall Enter First," and "Why Do the Heathen Rage."

She once wrote to a colleague, "Pornography and sentimentality and anything else in excess are all sins against form, and I think they ought to be approached as sins against art rather than sins against morality." Fiction is a way of seeing truth and enlarging the scope of human consciousness and spirituality. Her stories are about the South and Southern characters, rural and urban, and yet they are much more and that is why they endure.

Among her favorite authors were Henry James, Joseph Conrad and Nathaniel Hawthorne. She particularly admired Hawthorne's view that the writer deepens the mystery, and Conrad's aim of rendering the highest possible justice to the visible universe. She once wrote the following about fiction: "What offends my taste in fiction is when right is held up as wrong, or wrong as right. Fiction is the concrete expression of mystery — mystery that is lived." And later she wrote, "I'm mighty tired of reading reviews that call 'A Good Man...' brutal and sarcastic. The stories [her own short stories] are hard but they are hard because there is nothing harder or less sentimental than Christian realism."

O'Connor's work deals mightily with moral consequences for characters who try to acquire "respect" and the
price they pay for it in deception, self-delusion and dishon-
esty. Her moralism is heavily Christian and particularly
Catholic. She described herself as a believer in all Christian
doctrine. But, she also wrote, "any spiritual writer ought to
wear thin for you. It's like reading criticism of poetry all of the
time and not reading poetry." Commenting on a talk she was
to give to a Catholic women's group on the slurpy subject
"What Is a Wholesome Novel?" she wrote, "I intend to tell
them that the reason they find nothing but obscenity in
modern fiction is because that is all they know how to
recognize." She knew the difference between sincere
spiritual disciplines and outward pious nonsense. And she
was not very impressed with the "beat" writers of the late
fifties. "You can't trust them as poets either because they are
too busy acting like poets. The true poet is anonymous as to
his habits, but these boys have to look, act, and apparently
smell like poets." In another letter she wrote, "I doubtless
hate pious language worse than you because I believe the
realities it hides." She once read how Roy Rogers' horse had
attended a church service in Pasadena and the usual attendance doubled. Most important to her was that the horse
seemed to enjoy himself.

In response to a *Time* magazine editorial in 1956 that
complained about the negativity of American writers, she
replied to a friend, "I mortally and strongly defend the right
of an artist to select a negative aspect of the world to portray,
and as the world gets more materialistic there will be more
such to select from. Of course you are only enabled to know
what is black by having light to see it by, but that is no part of

the Luce contention.... The question is not is this negative or positive, but is it believable? The Luces say the negativeness of our novels is not believable because statistics tell us that we are rich and strong and democratic. In which case Dr. Kinsey and Dr. Gallup are sufficient for the day thereof."

Nor was she one to join protest movements or social-action groups. To an inquiry about supporting the feminist movement she replied, "On the subject of the feminist business, I just never think, that is never think of qualities which are specifically feminine or masculine. I suppose I divide people into two classes: the Irksome and the Non-Irksome without regard to sex. Yes, and there are the Medium Irksome and the Rare Irksome." Regarding race, "I should ride the bus more often. Once I heard the driver say to the rear occupants, 'All right, all you stovepipe blondes, git on back ther.' At that moment I became an integrationist."

In 1957 the General Electric Playhouse produced "The Life You Save May Be Your Own" in which Gene Kelly made his television debut. Incidentally, the host and producer of that series was Ronald Reagan. Here are some of O'Connor's responses. "Having witnessed his [Kelly's] performance I must say I am not overcome by his acting powers. We don't have a television but Sister [her aunt] in town does, so we went to see the play. Now I am double glad we don't have one. The best I can say for it is that conceivably it could have been worse. Just conceivably.... Several children stopped me on the street and complimented me. Dogs who live in houses with television have paused to sniff me. The local city fathers think I am now a credit to the community. One old lady said, 'That was a play that really made me think.' I didn't ask her what." She never sold any more stories for television production.

"Fiction is supposed to represent life, and the fiction writer has to use as many aspects of life as are necessary to make his total picture convincing. The fiction writer doesn't state, he shows, renders. It's the nature of fiction and it can't be helped. . . . All good stories are about conversion, about a character's changing . . . the action of grace changes a character. Grace can't be experienced in itself . . . all my stories are about the action of grace on a character who is not very willing to support it."

She accepted from Teilhard de Chardin what she had already learned herself, "passive diminishment" — the serene acceptance of afflictions and losses that are unchangeable. This acceptance led her finally to what the speaker in a famous Rilke poem, "Apollo," realized as he was drawn into the power of a sculpture he observed: "You must change your life."

With remarkable manner and courage she lived out her long and close association with death. For herein lies what makes her believable: her quest for truth is pure and we can trust her. She did not require or even allow her life to be interpreted by others, nor did she seek counsel in her dark times to see how she really felt. Her inner guide spoke from her soul and through her stories and her letters. She was a faithful listener and willing reporter. It is the softness of such inner voices obliterated by the noisy external world that keeps us far off the mark. We are caught in the din of our perpetually active lives. We cannot hear our own selves; or, if we do, we do not believe what we hear.

In 1955 she wrote "Lupus is one of the those diseases in the rheumatic department; it comes and goes; when it comes I retire and when it goes, I venture forth. My father had it some twelve or fifteen years ago, but at that time there was nothing for it but the undertaker; but now it can be controlled with ACTH. I have enough energy to write with, and as that is all I have any business doing anyhow, I can with one eye squinted take it all as a blessing. What you have to measure out, you come to observe closer, or so I tell myself."

In 1956 she developed a serious hip disorder, aseptic necrosis, perhaps. She wrote the following: "I'm informed it's crutches for me from now on out. Putting a cap on it [her hip] won't be possible because the bone is diseased. So, so much for that, I will henceforth be a structure with a flying buttress ... I am real awkward and there is always a crash going on behind me, but I am learning."

She also confided in 1956, "You are wrong that it was long ago I gave up thinking anything could be worked out on the surface. I have found it out, like everybody else, the hard way and only in the last two years as a result of, I think, two things, sickness and success. One of them alone wouldn't have done it for me, but the combination was guaranteed. I've never been anywhere but sick. In a sense sickness is a place, more instructive than a long trip to Europe, and it's always a place where there is no company, where nobody can follow. Sickness before death is a very appropriate thing, and I think those who don't have it miss one of God's mercies. Success is almost as isolating and nothing points out vanity as well. But the surface hereabouts has always been very flat. I come from a family where the only emotion respectable to show is irritation. In some this tendency produces hives, in others literature, in me, both." She never changed her views about either sickness or success.

Lupus usually follows a course of exacerbations and remissions and O'Connor's was no exception. In the end lupus is not a curable disease in this form, and it was inevitable that sooner or later, someone would try to get her to Lourdes. Despite her strong Catholic foundation she resisted. She simply did not want to go. However, when a seriously ill as well as wealthy relative made arrangements, all expenses covered, for the two of them to go, she had no graceful way out.

Despite the enormous drain on her already frail body she made the trip in 1958 and had an audience with the pope on the way back. Upon her return she wrote, "Lourdes was not as bad as I expected. I took the bath. From a selection of bad motives, such as to prevent any bad conscience for having not done it, and because it seemed at the time that it must be what was wanted for me. I went early in the morning. Only about forty ahead of me, so the water looked pretty clean. They passed around the water for les malades to drink and everybody drinks out of the same cup. As somebody said, 'The miracle is that the place don't bring on epidemics.' Well, I did it all and with very bad grace." Shortly after writing this, she learned that her hip had recalcified sufficiently for her to give up crutches. However, soon after, she fractured a rib during a fit of coughing. Her generous relative never improved and subsequently died, happy that O'Connor seemed to have benefited from the experience.

By the following spring she had to wear stockings, gloves, long dresses, and a hat to protect her skin from the sun. She continued on ACTH or cortisone and chloroquin. Despite setbacks and disappointments she continued to write three or four hours a day as well as maintain her extensive correspondence. Throughout all of this she seldom referred to her disease, except in passing terms. Once she noted that the steroids made her face look like that of one of the Chinese pheasant roosters she used to raise. Despite her faith in miracles, she never felt deserted by God because she was not healed. She did not pretend to know the mind of God.

On the subject of God she wrote, "There is a question whether faith can or is supposed to be emotionally satisfying. I must say that the thought of everyone lolling around in an emotionally satisfying faith is repugnant to me ... what people don't realize is how much religion costs. They think faith is a big electric blanket, when of course it is the cross. It is much better to believe than not to believe. If you feel you can't believe, you must at least do this: keep an open mind." Another time she confessed, "But let me tell you this: faith comes and goes. It rises and falls like tides of an invisible ocean."

As the years passed, she maintained her good cheer and never fell into profound depression nor just stoically hung on to a fragment of her life. She wrote, "As far as I am concerned as long as I can get at that typewriter, I have enough. They expect me to improve, or so they say. I expect anything that happens."

Eventually she developed a seriously bleeding uterine fibroid. Her physicians debated the risks of surgery causing an exacerbation of the lupus. In February 1964 she wrote, "Well it looks like I am going to arrive at the cutting table before you. The medication is doing fine, but I have a large tumor, and if they don't make haste and get rid of it they will have to remove me and leave it."

The surgery was performed, and it was more than she could withstand. Her lupus did indeed flare up in a malignant form and she suffered from anemia, infection and renal failure. Despite all of this, she was able to write the following after three weeks in the hospital: "It sure don't look like I'll ever get out of this joint. By now I know all the student nurses who want to write — if they are sloppy and inefficient and can't make up a bed, that's them — they want to write. 'Inspirational stuff I'm good at,' said one of them. 'I just get so taken up with it I forget what I'm writing.'"

She finally made it home, but she sensed her time was short. "So far as I can see the medicine and the disease run neck in neck to kill you." Yet she still had the time and wit to respond to an English professor who wrote inquiring about his classes' analysis of her work. "As for Mrs. May, I must have named her that because I knew some English teacher would write and ask why. I think you folks sometimes strain the soup too thin." On July 5, 1964 she confided to Sister Mariella Gable, "The wolf, I'm afraid, is inside tearing up the place [*lupus* is Latin for "wolf"]. I've been in the hospital fifty days already this year. At present I'm just home from the hospital and have to stay in bed. I have an electric typewriter and I write a little every day, but I'm not allowed to do much."

Flannery O'Connor died peacefully at home in her own bed on August 3, 1964.

The Beckoning

I HAVE commuted the last twelve years from Bainbridge Island to my office in Seattle by ferry. During the busy times, there are hundreds of other commuters engrossed in reading papers, magazines and books. I've made mental notes of what they select to read as they make the trip.

Most choose a local newspaper, usually surveying headlines first, sports page or comics next, and lastly the journalism for which the newspaper was intended in the first place. There are Bible readers often looking a bit embarrassed. An occasional Christian Scientist with Mary Baker Eddy in hand carries out some particular study. Stockbrokers glare at pictures of successful stern-faced men on the covers of business magazines, the promises of glistening investment brochures, the intricacies of financial statements and stock offerings, or the gospel according to Iacocca.

Lawyers peruse depositions, making notes in the margins. Engineers pore over the diagrams in technical magazines, while doctors nod off over medical journals. Gardeners study new methods of slug destruction. Fashion magazines with sultry, underfed women and athletic men with wind-blown hair and arrogant stares hopelessly outclass their readers. Popular-fiction readers have settled on a few of the current best sellers, but their eyes are not as wide with excitement as the sensual pictures on the book covers predict.

Now and then I see a friend whose interest is history wading through an esoteric book on Greeks or Celts. He works for the government as a processor of small-business loans and always wears the same battered hat. He is a marker buoy at the harbor entrance for the almost extinct serious voyager through the works of any poet, of Kierkegaard or Nietzche, of the heavy novels of Thomas Hardy, of the charming essays of Lewis Thomas, of the biographies of Thomas Merton, Theodore Roosevelt or Virginia Woolf.

A few months ago I had lunch with a colleague who had just purchased *The Complete Works of Ralph Waldo Emerson.* The middle-aged family doctor who practiced in a suburb outside of Seattle had heard the voice of the mighty Emerson calling through a quotation cited by someone else. The good doctor dashed off to a proper bookstore where he found the volume he showed me. Will he become an Emerson scholar? I don't know, but I doubt that he will. What Emerson has for him is personal and part of his life right now. If others listen carefully they may hear Emerson's voice as well.

There is a beckoning that comes from the written words of those who search long and hard within themselves and set forth for us what we too may be searching for without yet realizing. The same beckoning is part of the gift of all artistic or creative endeavors that send signals to receptors deep inside us. The part of our minds that worries about appearance and money tells us that what we feel is a childish fantasy and has no place in grownups. These beckonings are similar to dreams trying to rouse us in the night in order that we might record their images, confusing stories, preposterous sequence and immoral content. If we record our dreams and consider them later, we may find to our surprise that they enhance us in ways we never considered possible.

One version of what is inside of us is in the following poem from *The Kabir Book*, poems of the fifteenth-century poet Kabir who exemplified the ecstatic poetry of the Hindus and Sufis. The translation is by Robert Bly, and the poem is taken from a section entitled "The Fish In the Sea Is Not Thirsty." Listen to what our receptors are like when we are described as clay jugs.

> Inside this clay jug there are canyons and pine
> mountains, and the maker of canyons and
> pine mountains.
> All seven oceans are inside, and hundreds of millions of
> stars.
> The acid that tests gold is there, and the one who judges
> jewels.
> And the music from the strings no one touches, and the
> source of all water.
>
> If you want the truth, I will tell you the truth:
> Friend, listen: the God whom I love is inside.

How much more wonderful is this poem than the vagaries of anxiety, depression and happiness. I don't know what happiness looks like, but I know what a pine-covered mountain looks like, and why there must be an acid to test gold.

PART FOUR

The Narrow Ridge

Preparing for the Opera

THE afternoon breeze carries its prophecy of spring rain as I hurry to finish my work. My wife and I have been firstnighters at the Seattle Opera since it began. She's a singer and I'm an admirer. Tonight the opera is *Tosca,* in which Scarpia is stabbed to death by Tosca, who jumps to her death from the parapet after Cavaradossi is killed by a firing squad. The opera ends because all the characters are dead.

Meanwhile, I'm farming. My project is a new pen for Bruce, my boar. The success of the pen depends upon Bruce being as afraid of electricity as I am. I set metal poles, attach insulators, and about eighteen inches above the ground string wire which connects to a transformer. I snap on the switch and receive a painful jolt when I grab the wrong end of the current-tester.

Meanwhile, Bruce complains from the boarded stall in the barn. I've tried for the past several weeks to let Bruce live in the orchard where he could root out blackberries and enjoy the fresh air. He refused to stay inside the perimeter fence. At night he would snap off the two-by-fours with his snout, shoulder his huge carcass through the opening and meander into the barn where he gorged himself on horse feed. I'd hear him snorting from my bedroom, and I'd scramble into my robe and slippers and chase him back to the orchard with a stick. He always went back without a fuss. But, like some people I've met, Bruce is guided by his gastrointestinal tract and his genitals. The sow has a new brood and there is only food left for Bruce.

He is about four hundred percent larger than when I bought him at an auction in Marysville to breed to our sow. She was about four hundred percent larger than Bruce at the time. He was willing, even inspired, but he couldn't reach. Some neighbors suggested he stand on a box. The veterinarian advised we dig a ditch for the sow to stand in. That way we could raise "furrow-bred hogs." While Bruce was growing up, he often looked unwell. I suspected he had headaches in addition to insomnia. With lots of food and time, Bruce became a successful sire. Now he weighs six hundred pounds or better.

He and I have a mutual understanding. I respect him because of his size and strength and he has no interest in me at all. It is not that he dislikes me, he just prefers to ignore me. I think he blames me for his early days of frustration.

I have not fed Bruce all day. My plan is to entice him with a bucket of grain and lead him to his new home. I lean over the boarded stall and rub his bristly head. He gazes up at me, his beady eyes almost hidden by his huge ears. I admire his gigantic shoulders and his prehistoric tusks. I'm thankful that within his ferocious appearance beats the heart of a coward.

Using words of profane encouragement, I lead Bruce the hundred feet or so to his new pen by waving the bucket of grain under his nose. Once he is inside I close the wire gate. Bruce spins around, knows he has been tricked and sniffs the wire while I fumble to turn on the switch.

He lurches forward, jerking the wire with his snout and pulling out a nearby post. He is free and off in a jerky trot toward the mud in a long drainage ditch. I'm furious as I grab a long stick and whack him in the rump. That is poor strategy. He grunts and picks up the pace. He can run a lot faster than I can. I chase him around the manure-strewn pasture while the horses watch.

After falling in the mud and rolling part way down a rise, I'm ready to make Bruce into bacon. Off we go, zigzagging across the pasture. Bruce stays ahead, but I get in a good poke now and then.

Soon I am winded and footsore as well as fuming and filthy. Bruce tires too. The afternoon sun has broken through and neither of us is a distance runner. Bruce flops down in the mud and lies on his right side puffing and grunting. He stares one-eyed at me and pleads for mercy. I kneel down next to him and splash muddy water over his huge frame. My wife calls out that I should quit playing with Bruce and get ready for the opera. Bruce and I have a common bond: we are both misunderstood, Bruce by me, and me by my wife. At least my wife doesn't have twelve offspring at a crack, although Bruce doesn't have to support his.

We both regain our wind after a few moments, and as a gesture of good sportsmanship, I goose Bruce with my stick and give him a head start. He runs a short way and turns toward his new pen. I replace the post, add another strand of wire and connect the electricity. Bruce begins to dig a rut to sleep in as he roots around in the brush.

My wife and I have to settle for hamburgers and rush down the aisle as the lights dim for Act One.

Killers

What is man without the beasts? If all beasts were gone, man would die from a great loneliness of spirit. For whatever happens to the beasts soon happens to man. All things are connected.

Chief Seattle

THE terrible decline in the number of wild creatures throughout the world is beyond my power to envision, despite warnings from concerned people who seek protection for endangered species and intelligent use of the others. Avarice remains the driving force behind the legal arguments and public-relations brochures designed to mollify those worried about the slaughter and to discredit the rebels who will not remain silent.

The Canadian writer and naturalist, Farley Mowat, perhaps best known for *Never Cry Wolf* and *A Whale for the Killing,* which were both made into successful movies, published a complex and compelling work, *Sea of Slaughter.* An indication of this book's importance and accuracy is that Mowat was denied a visa to the United States, where he hoped to promote his book. The reasons for the denial were couched in bureaucratic sawdust, but the real reason is his painstaking indictment of all countries that participated in the massive devastations of fishes, birds, shellfish, land and sea mammals along the North Atlantic seaboard over the past five hundred years, and those countries that continue to do so today. Mowat believes that we cannot wash the bloody stains from our collective hands through documentation. But we can stop the wholesale harvest of the remaining creatures as the means to make fortunes.

I bought *Sea of Slaughter* while on a short vacation in Canada one summer. Mowat is deservedly popular in his country and the book was prominently displayed in stores. I was unable to read more than a few pages at a sitting and even that much didn't fit well with the indulgences of a holiday. Yet I found myself pulled back again and again through chapter after tragic chapter, and I was reminded how several years earlier I accumulated notes and read much about the Nazi death camps only to find that I had no proper viewpoint, nor could I exploit that material for my own satisfaction. The presence of evil dripped everywhere and the innocents, nameless and too easily forgotten, shuffled through my conscience.

A similar dark void of suffering gathered around me again when I read Mowat, not because the slaughter of creatures is equal on the moral scale to the slaughter of people. But it is a lot closer than we would like to think. I belong to the race of all-time champion killers, the human race. When we are not efficient enough with our natural cunning and bodies, we devise weapons whose consequences we cannot predict and too easily ignore when they become known. I remember an interview with the brother of the late

J. Robert Oppenheimer, the father of the Manhattan Project. He recounted how, when he and Robert learned of the Hiroshima bombing, they first cried, "Thank God it worked!" and a moment later, "What have we done?"

The Faustian bargain is peculiarly human, for only we who can abstract and plan the future are capable of giving up our souls or, if you prefer, innermost integrity, in favor of the pursuit of power, wealth and knowledge. We believe that the next set of accomplishments will solve the conflicts produced by the present set of accomplishments. For example, there is the physician who sacrifices family for professional success only to learn later that his loved ones had suffered, not benefitted, from his accomplishments.

The forces of evil depend upon human greed and excessive confidence in our abilities coupled with the poorly understood and biologically inaccurate concept of survival of the fittest. Another Canadian writer, Robertson Davies, put it in different terms by pointing out that not only God hears and answers our prayers.

But what of my own participation in killing? The exterminator recently fumigated my cabin, which had become inhabited by carpenter ants. I swept up the carcasses and disposed of them. The next morning I tromped the gravelled and muddy beach, shovel in one hand and bucket in the other, as I feretted out steamer clams which would later bubble in the hot oven until they were dead and succulent. Fillets of fish cool in my refrigerator alongside the squeezed pulp of severed oranges. Whether the cow who gave the milk still lives, I do not know, nor do I much care.

The cows, clams and oranges will not revolt. The oceans cannot reclaim their once teeming variety of fishes and mammals, nor dissolve the pollutants that resist chemical breakdown and alter the transformation of matter into new life.

I stand, stretch and peer out the rain-streaked windows. I cannot even see the bay, or for that matter the trees eight feet in front of the deck. For all I know, everything I cannot see disappears until I see it again. But the clams cannot escape and I can take as many as I am willing to work for. The clams have nothing to say about that. Let them enjoy their filtering and spurting one more night.

Even in this refuge from what makes my life complicated and causes me worry, I cannot separate myself more than briefly from the fuming world that is not of my making. Sometimes I propose analyses or offer solutions that others consider to be meddling, idiocy or psychosis, especially when I argue from more than one point of view or change my mind. If I set aside the need to argue with others' opinions of me, I can devote my attention to my own concerns. E.B. White wrote that it is time-consuming to have enemies.

I cannot speak for others, but it is only by meddling that I find out what is there, only by idiocy that I can become intelligent and only by psychosis that I can find the sanities in my life where all things connect.

Fading is the order of this day. Sunlight fading over the Olympics. Dim light dulled by cedar walls fading in this cabin. The year fading. No deaths among my loved ones during the past twelve months, but we had two close calls. Last spring our fifteen-year-old son rode out the flip of a sports car driven by one of his friends. The car levelled its top along with the hood and trunk except for one corner on the driver's side. Neither boy was belted in and the centrifugal force of the roll threw both of them safely on the floor. They scrambled out the only available window with cuts, bruises and fright as the price they paid.

Earlier my wife had escaped death or serious injury when her car was struck on the driver's side by a car coming toward her that skidded in the gravel and torpedoed across the center line. She was belted in. In her unflappable manner she exchanged information with the other driver, hitched a ride to the church and rehearsed her choir as scheduled. Four serious accidents in less than two years for our family, each time only minor injuries. The odds are against us in the next one. I hold that thought as the wind shudders past the cabin.

Others have not been so lucky. A late-night phone call from a relative. One of his sons, thirty, married, father of two, prime of life, killed himself with a pistol shot to the head. Those who knew him thought he was fine. There were the usual speculations: broken home, business reverses, chemical imbalance in his brain.

A man in his twenties stops at the night-deposit box of a local bank with the proceeds of the business he manages. Another man, younger, presses a Magnum revolver against the first man's throat and squeezes the trigger. An instant and painless death. In many ways better than some of the other possibilities from bullet wounds to the brain and spinal cord. A murder conviction is small consolation, because justice never has replaced such a loss.

A rainy fall night, slick and winding roads, a fast car with three teen-agers inside hits a ditch. The sixteen-year-old girl in the back is thrown out and crushed to death when the car rolls on top of her. A seatbelt might have saved her, but that possibility only makes solace that much harder to come by. Traffic details are of more interest to the police and insurance companies than to her family and close friends.

Where is the fairness in all of this? Killers come in noise

or silence as the case may be, and sooner or later, there is one for each of us.

I am alarmed at my gloom as the twilight gathers around this small cabin. It is hard to tell what is real in this half-light, half-dark. Dreaming with my eyes open, I sense what is beyond my senses.

Presences are here now. Those taken by killers nestle close, as if I send out a single bell tone that meets another and now I cannot tell them apart. A pure note hangs in the room. I hear that voice that has no speech: Am I an analyzer or a part of life? This is the question asked by the holy days at the winter's solstice.

"What's wrong will always be wrong," states the voice of one of my frequent dream visitors, poet Richard Hugo.

"I would have taken this road on sight, not knowing who lived along it, not knowing where, if anywhere it goes." Hugo again. He sustains me once more in dark times. The lonely road of life is as it should be, for out of loneliness comes purpose.

Later, I stand at the top of the beach stairs. The wind has quit. The bay is quiet. The tide has come home. All days are holy. All life is holy. All things are holy. When reveries are heard it is because someone listens. In the winter moonlight I can make out the landing at the bottom of the stairs, the edge of the water below the reliable bulkhead and logs still in place after the storm. Stars are everywhere in the sky, my shivers are gone and I am ready for the holy days.

Rearview Mirror

THE country night is peaceful and there are no other cars on the road. I drive a comfortable forty-five in my VW diesel sedan and listen to the baseball game on the radio. The Mariners are losing in the late innings. The May air is cool and refreshing as it rushes through the car window. I am alone and I watch for deer while the deep gloom ahead of me brightens from my headlights and closes in behind me as I pass.

My rearview mirror catches the lights of a speeding car and I notice that in addition to its four headlights it has two spotlights mounted on the front bumper. Soon the car is a few feet from my rear bumper and all six lights flood my car with brilliance. I change the angle of the rearview mirror but that doesn't help much.

We come to a stop sign and I make a left turn and drive the posted twenty-five miles per hour through the small town. The other car does the same with only two headlights showing and those are on low beam. I make another left turn and start down the Chimacum Valley toward the Hood Canal Bridge. The road is two lanes of blacktop with no shoulders, and deserted except for occasional farm houses. I get nervous when I see that the other car follows me.

This stretch of road is several miles long. The other car closes up, then backs off. I hold my speed at sixty and I have no illusions about outrunning any car with the one I am driving. Suddenly the other car races up behind me and snaps on all six lights, making me a fully illuminated target. I speed up and the other driver does the same. After two or three miles of this I touch my brakes, and as he backs off he flips his lights on and off several times.

At least he is a reasonable distance behind me and I try to relax and pick up my speed. I've never noticed before how lonely this road is at night although I've travelled it many times. The ball games ends. I push in a tape of a Mozart symphony and turn up the volume, filling the car with music.

The other car accelerates and passes me on my left with all six of its lights glaring. I hold my speed and stay back as far as I can. I roll up the windows and lock the doors. The other car slows, and I do too. I keep my lights on low beam and I can see two men in the front seat. Our speed diminishes and soon we are at thirty-five and still slowing. I signal to pass, but the other car swerves in front of me when I try to go around and will not let me by. I've never seen this car before. I'm sure I don't know its occupants and I don't wish to get acquainted now. I consider my options.

Obscene gestures are not for cowards like me when I'm in a tight spot. If only I had my battered three-quarter-ton pickup, I'd climb on their rear bumper and move them along. At least I think I would. I consider what I have in my car to use as weapons. There are several books of philosophy and poetry as well as a novel or two. I decide reading to them will not help. My only hammer is my rubber-headed reflex hammer. My briefcase is filled with medical charts and journals. There is a small bag of laundry and a flashlight. If worst comes to worst, I will have to count on the flashlight.

In spite of my heroic fantasies I am not a fighter. And even if I were, there are two of them and there is no help in sight. I don't know about their physical characteristics, but I do know mine. Accounts of motorists being robbed and beaten, or murdered, flood my thoughts.

If only I had Barrymore, my son Kurt's aggressive pit bull who can eat a Doberman for lunch and is a fearless protector. Besides, he loves to fight. A fighter must not mind pain and disfigurement. I hate both. If the fight goes badly for Barrymore, all he asks is a rematch.

If only I were a powerful athlete. As a boy I read how the driver of one car challenged the driver of another to a fight. The man who climbed out to defend himself was Joe Louis, the heavyweight champ. The first man recognized him and ran away.

This is not the time to be philosophical, but that's the way my mind works, especially when I'm angry or frightened. The pen may be mightier than the sword but I don't know how that would help right now. I feel moisture under my arms and across my brow. The men in the car ahead do not look back. They have me trapped.

If only I had a can of Mace, except with my luck I'd face it backwards when I cut loose. If only I had the small tear-gas gun my father carried in his shirt pocket when he was a police detective. It resembled a large fountain pen and held a sealed shell the size of a .410-gauge shotgun shell. A snap of the release and your opponent was reduced to coughs, gags and tears.

If only I had my father here in his prime.

This is getting serious. I know there are a lot of creeps around and two of them are after me. We continue our slow pace on this deserted road and I wonder what their intentions are.

If only I had my revolver. It is a .38 Colt and it knows how to kill. Etched in the metal between the cylinder and the handgrip is a date, 1/7/52, and above it, some initials. My father marked the gun so that he could identify it in court as the murder weapon used by a man to shoot his wife. After the trial the judge gave him the gun and later he gave it to me. I've shot it many times, but the gun has shot no one else, although no doubt it remembers what to do when someone pulls the trigger.

Could I get angry enough or frightened enough to shoot another person? For me, anger and fear are related and I can go from one to the other in a moment. Would I temporize and miss my chance to gain the upper hand? What if I misjudged the seriousness of the situation and shot a prankster instead of a dangerous person? In being a physician, I've seen lots of people die, but that's not the same as drawing a bead and killing someone.

The minutes drag as if they are pulled one after the other. Maybe these guys are afraid of me. Maybe they think I'm waiting for them to try something. For that thought I am thankful. I shift into second gear. We crawl along at fifteen.

Coming into view behind me are the lights of other night travellers. My hopes soar. The driver ahead also sees them and screeches away, leaving me far behind. The first car honks as he passes me on my way to forty. I rev the VW to the top and follow that car at seventy and keep the second one behind me. I stay between the two of them until we cross the bridge.

I turn right off the bridge, roll down the window and head for home. Even though I am safe, I keep glancing in the rearview mirror.

A Time Alone

ONCE more I am where I live best, at my cabin by the sea. It is a cold February night and snow filters through the heavy air. The fireplace crackles and the comfortable cedar logs creak in reply. On clear nights the Point Wilson lighthouse is visible from the deck. Tonight my visual system reports the lighthouse is no longer there. It is obscured by snow. On this same deck are clams and oysters which I gathered by flashlight from the beach a short time ago. The nap I took earlier left me with a crick in my neck. My supper was salad, cold chicken and hot tea. I've looked forward to these three days alone. My wife knows I need this time.

Loneliness has nothing to do with being alone. I've never gotten used to loneliness: the sense of loss with the passing of a person or experience, such as a child's first steps, or the reliable love from someone important in my life.

The oysters are for lunch tomorrow and I will eat them alone. They were to be shared with my father who died in early January. In the final stages of his illness he asked me to bring him oysters from this beach which he loved so much. He would say, "I know they are not on my diet, but maybe a few, pan-fried, wouldn't hurt anything." I didn't make this trip in time.

Tonight I am far from those dear, dying people who struggle each day, and even with the best health insurance on their side, will lose. Sometimes as a doctor I don't know what to say to them, and as patients they don't know what to say to me. We look at each other with moist eyes and helpless smiles. At those moments I feel as though I have spent my life studying neurology and it is all for nothing. One day I may be told by someone that my biological self is beyond repair. I hope that doctor will understand I won't mind so much if I can hear him clear his throat as we talk.

In this severe life, I ask myself about beauty and truth. A bone scan showing widespread metastases is not beauty or truth. It is a documentation of our frailty and may become a reportable case, or microfilmed and labeled "Teaching File." The occurrence of something that is true is not truth, and beauty is more than what pleases our senses. We physicians cannot find truth or beauty by concerning ourselves with only public relations, fiscal responsibility, medical audits, clinic and hospital architecture, procedure manuals, and continuing medical education. These necessary items should never be given more than their appropriate amount of worth.

I recall watching a mentally deficient man wash the marble wall in front of a hospital elevator. His movements were slow and awkward as he squinted through thick glasses and wrinkled his nose to keep his glasses from sliding down. When I stepped out of the elevator a while later I could see he was finishing his work. He smiled as he viewed the immaculately clean marble wall. He and the wall had need of each other and both were better because of this experience.

I carry more wood in from the woodshed under the collapsing garage built forty years ago. The snow falls harder and silence is broken only by my puffing and my steps crunching the snow. Back inside the cabin I think back to my childhood fantasies of living in the far north with Buck, my wonder dog, who would give his life for me. Together we could survive all of nature's arctic violence. I could snowshoe endless miles, survive on snow and courage, and kill wolves with my knife if that was all I had to fight with.

Once, in a fit of heroic enthusiasm, I decided to turn out for high school football. I was fourteen, almost six feet tall and weighed one hundred thirty-eight pounds, most of which was bones. My ears stuck out like car doors with my crew cut, and I was so myopic I couldn't see the scoreboard unless I was right next to it. When I pitched for a local baseball team I missed most of the catcher's signals. He thought I was just dumb.

I couldn't do a single pushup, and I was last in every sprint. And that was without football gear, which of course I'd never worn. The only reason I went back to practice the second day was because I didn't want to be ridiculed by the gruff coach who loved to make examples out of quitters.

Kenny, a small boy who played shortstop on our baseball team, had visions of being a halfback. After a long drill of calisthenics, we lined up for a blocking drill. Most of those who would make the team had already been issued uniforms. The rest of us watched. Kenny blocked a huge kid named Ron, who was later killed while a marine in the Korean War. Kenny hit Ron with all his might and they both went down. Ron scrambled up under his own power. Kenny lay on the grass in the hot September sun and tried to be brave. The coach yelled, "Atta boy, Kenny!"

At the first chance to be in a passing drill, I pulled up lame, an acute cramp in my courage, or a sudden revelation in my insight. I cursed my luck, and promised to turn out next year. I limped back to the dressing room where I was ignored by the coach and consoled by my friends. Of course I never turned out for football again. My mother was greatly relieved, which made matters worse.

The hum of the refrigerator stops. The snow falls in an impenetrable blanket. Silence surrounds me. It is as if I will receive an important message. I have no reason to leave this chair. I remember the way my father used to stroke his nose with his right index finger when he sat in his favorite chair and contemplated. And of years ago when his fellow officers in the Seattle Police Department told me how proud he was to have a son who wanted to be a doctor. And how many times we disappointed each other and how during his later years we became closer.

The Narrow Ridge

I

IT IS difficult for me to think through many of the dilemmas of medical practice and purpose during the tensions of my daily work as a physician. This is one reason why I often withdraw to my special place, my cabin by the sea. Here my life slows down and I feel a part of all that is around me and within me. My left brain gives up its incessant analyzing and my thinking slows to the pace of trees, wind and waves.

The art of medicine is a subtle art that is hard to acquire and difficult to sustain. It is not the ability to handle difficult patients, make brilliant diagnoses or perform heroic surgery. It is not related to diplomas and postgraduate education. The art of medicine includes the mathematics of both biology and art, where things do not add up to larger sums of the same things. Instead, there is a bringing forth of new and different things and experiences, a process of fertilization, conception and birthing.

I think of the differences and the similarities between

the fields of music and medicine and the work of pianists and physicians. Both must master the scientific structure upon which their work is built. Long periods of study are spent learning technical skills without which neither the expert performance of music nor the expert practice of medicine is possible. Without people who have talent, ambition, discipline and dedication there would be no pianists or physicians.

The composers of music and the scientists who develop medical advances seldom witness the life their work takes on and where it goes. That is left to pianists and physicians. Listening to one of Artur Rubinstein's recordings may fill our emptiness or still our fear and give us pleasure or courage. The same is true of loving care given to us by a compassionate physician.

Being able to read the tiny notes written on a score and knowing the anatomy of the human body make possible the arts of music and medicine. It does not ensure them, but it makes them possible. Staring at a Chopin score does not teach me to play it. I don't read music. In the same way, staring at the pages of an electroencephalogram would not have helped Rubinstein make a proper interpretation and give cogent advice to a patient.

Rubinstein said that pianists should not play music that does not speak to them. Similarly, phisicians should not care for patients unless they want to hear what the patients have to say. Not just their words, but their voices, their true voices. Sometimes I wonder, when patients speak to me, what they are trying to say. And when I answer, counsel, advise, what I am trying to say to them. It is often easy for me to anticipate what my patients will say because the clinical histories for certain neurological disorders are predictable. There are only so many verbs and adjectives with which to describe a pinched nerve in the neck or a slight stroke.

The light-hearted banter of our early conversation may cloud the terror of what the patient fears or knows. I ask patients how they are and they often unthinkingly answer fine. My next question is, "What are you doing here, then?" Or when the spouse accompanies the patient, I say that now I will hear the truth about the symptoms. Even after long experience, I can get carried away with social conversation and the patient has to bring me back to the point of the visit.

I must not avoid what my patients want or need to say and do not know how to. Sometimes I can tell that my patient is near tears and will break down if I ask one more question. Maybe I don't want to face that on a morning when I am discouraged myself. Yet I know what I should do. If my patients want to wave me off, they can. But I should always be interested in whatever disturbs them even if it is not within my specialized field. It may not be the primary reason they are in my office, but I should be interested.

We have few places where, and times when, we can speak honestly and confidentially to each other. One reason why we have so many counsellors and psychotherapists is that we are a nation of talkers and not listeners. Physicians should be listeners. If my office is not a place for my patient to be heard, then where?

We physicians are at our best when we and our patients blend together our external lives of perceptions and principles with our inner lives of memories, characters and souls. We are at our worst when we don't. Most often we are somewhere in between.

Most physicians possess the capacity for humanness, but

we are under pressures from the high priests of business and the cohorts of bureaucracy to conform to generally accepted rules that usually work against us as individuals trying to become more than we are. This is a serious problem and its resolution is difficult. Each of us has to decide where his or her true loyalty lies. If enough of us choose people over abstract corporate enterprise, there is within our profession the vigor and intelligence to improve life in general and human life in particular.

One day a colleague arranged for us to have lunch together at a Chinese restaurant. He was concerned about his nursing-home patients and wondered how much of what he did for them in the name of medical therapy and prolonging life was in their best interest. When and how does one make decisions that carry such consequences as these? He knew of my long-standing interest in these issues. He wanted discussion, maybe advice and understanding. Our lunch was excellent, our discussion lively and my fortune cookie carried the message, "Ignorance never solved a problem."

That lunch conversation, coupled with the deaths of several patients I'd recently been involved with, started me thinking about biological houses, the ones we physicians service and repair in our work. Every one of us begins in a womb and ends up inhabiting a diseased or broken biological house. We share these two universal experiences and all that can go wrong in between.

There is something degrading about a physician referring to "the stroke in 418," because it causes us to forget the personality that can no longer be recognized behind that damaged brain. Conventional wisdom may say that such persons are better off dead. But those are individual, personal decisions that should not be made on the basis of diagnosis alone. The dignity of the impaired should not be debased.

We in medicine are tempted to regard ourselves as above and beyond ordinary people and thus ordained to decide matters of life and death. Even worse, we may neglect matters of life and death by refusing to resolve our own conflicts about living and dying. Some of us beg off by applying every possible technique to avoid the moment of death, leaving it to nature, God or fate. Some of us hide behind the wonders of science, the barricades of large institutions, the sanctity of research or the principles of cost containment. Such attitudes determine what care we give to all from the tiniest premature infants to aged, bed-ridden seniles.

The ambiguity persists: the individual versus society, sacrificing a few to save many. Military metaphors dominate our thinking. We destroy populations of malignant cells, rebuild defenses, attack diseases, build therapeutic armamentariums, fight the invasions of cancer.

We are bullied by such language. If we could move away from it we might re-envision our work. We could become among those who rise up with praise for life, love for children, honor for each other and curiosity for mysteries not yet experienced.

In *Pilgrimage to Humanity* Albert Schweitzer writes:

I will buy from the Africans a young fish eagle which they have caught on a sandbank. But then I have to decide whether to let it starve or daily kill so many small fish in order to keep it alive. I decide for the latter course. Every day, however, I am oppressed by the fact that I am responsible for the sacrifice of one life for another.... The ethics of the reverence for life arises from real thinking and continuous relationship with reality.... The ethics of the reverence for life is the world-wide ethics of love. It is the ethics of Jesus.

At times, I am relieved when a particular patient dies. My outward statement is thankfulness for the blessed relief for both patient and family. My inner statement, the one that usually comes at night, is that I couldn't take much more myself and I'm glad my burden has been lifted. In the quiet of my cabin at the water's edge I consider whether I have the proper reverence for life.

II

There is no way for me to separate the care of patients from the care of my own life and still practice medicine as I should. The admonition, "Physician, heal thyself!" ruthlessly applies to me. When I stand on one side of the abyss, free from emotional involvement and empathy, and hurl treatment across to the afflicted on the other side it is a moral sin against my patients. It is also an easy sin for me to commit.

It begins, as I have said, when I stop listening to those who seek me out as a physician. It worsens when I put them off with pat answers. It gets worse yet when I forget how to say "I don't know." I may resort to such trickery as explaining away symptoms that I do not recognize as being psychosomatic in origin, which the patient takes to mean imaginary.

Without proper attention to my work, I may ascend the heights of arrogance by doubting that the patient has any symptoms at all. This is not to say that I should accept that the patient's own explanations and assessments are always correct. After all, patients can be just as manipulative as physicians when there are large stakes. There will always be the patient with an injury caused by someone whose insurance company can afford a large payoff, or one with the possibility of a disability pension if the injury is serious enough and the patient is tired of working at a job that represents failure or frustration. But even in these cases, I must remind myself that my task is not to debate the reality of my patients' complaints. The symptoms belong to my patients and not to me, and my patients can tell my any tales they wish. My task is to listen, question, examine, formulate a differential diagnosis, apply appropriate diagnostic techniques and come to a clinical assessment. Any time I don't do that, I have not been the physician I want to be and should be for my patients.

Both patients and I have to watch ourselves for evidence of consistency and inconsistency. I remember a woman who returned to see me after some twenty years for re-evaluation of headaches that were refractory to all treatments. She said that her headaches might have been bad before, but now they were intolerable. I reviewed her medical file and read back to her the description of her headaches that she had given me on her first visit. She had characterized them with exactly the same words as those she now used. According to the details of her history, nothing had changed. To her the headaches must have become much worse, but they sounded like the same headaches to me. A few days later, a woman whose case is medically quite complicated scolded me for suggesting that she had a viral infection every time I couldn't figure out the cause of her new symptoms. She said I told her the same thing several times a year, and nobody has that many viral infections. She was right.

Over the years I have heard far too many patients complain that their physicians never hear them out, and these are not just the occasional patients who have interminable medical histories. It does strain my patience when I realize that a particular patient will talk for however long I am willing to listen. I learned a way to control that problem from one of my partners. He tells such patients that forty-five minutes have been allotted for taking the medical history, and during that time they can talk about whatever they choose. I do the same thing and it seems fair to both the patients and myself. If more time is needed we schedule another appointment.

Although I cannot possibly help every patient who comes to me, at least I can be attentive to their reasons for being in my office. But it is difficult for me to maintain that standard. As a sinner in this respect I need frequent confession, forgiveness and redemption.

III

I was raised in a strict Protestant church. We believed that the world had been rejected by God because of the Fall of Man in the Garden of Eden. In order to escape the fires of damnation we each made a personal decision to accept Christ as our Savior. We believed the Bible was literally true despite overwhelming evidence to the contrary. God, being who he was, could make anything happen no matter how implausible it might be to us. And he was under no obligation to be consistent. As his followers, we avoided the goings-on in the world as much as possible. Our principle product was piety.

Most of those that I grew up with in that faith have slipped away or, if they still attend, their beliefs are not nearly so fiery as they once were. There are others for whom that system continues to provide comfort, security and hope. Those are not bad things.

However, I could not stay with any system that viewed itself as final, where all answers were known and where there was no place for my intractable curiosity and a boundless imagination, which constantly put me in a different place than where I was. As a boy, a walk through the woods became a jungle excursion for me. A night at my cousins' house was a trip to a foreign land. When I attended Cub Scout meetings, I was in the cavalry in my blue shirt and yellow neckerchief. I preferred to be anything other than what I was. For years I held myself in check, led prayer meetings, preached at missions, taught Sunday School and tried to keep my anemic faith alive.

But I could not sustain that faith and neither could God. I drifted loose from the trappings, but could not free myself of spiritual longings. Theodore Roethke wrote, "The race from God is the longest race of all." It was for me. But the either/or propositions allowed me no possibility for anything new. One was either man or woman, communist or capitalist, Democrat or Republican, saved or lost.

There was a new age appearing and I was overwhelmed by the relative theology that many people now applied to Christianity. Many previously firm tenets degenerated into matters of opinion. Dogma was dismissed, but often replaced by nothing except fancies, often superficial, even trite. The emphasis shifted from worship and acceptance to encounter groups and emotional discussions where people "got out their feelings." If I didn't like someone I should speak up, and that person was supposed to benefit from this enlightenment. Often they just said something like, "Stuff it, Bob!"

I was uncomfortable in this setting. I felt guilty about

trying not to feel guilty. Besides, I hated sitting on the floor and detested herb tea. Some of the groups found their way into orgies and the bliss of drugs. The groups I was in never did. Maybe that's why I lost interest.

In the sixties several of us ran a coffeehouse which had been started by a young minister in a forward-thinking church. In those days, subjects like abortion, euthanasia, draft resistance and premarital sex were off limits in more conventional settings. We had a high time flaunting the current standards with pithy aphorisms and long-winded dissertations. I was not wise enough to realize that I was concocting answers to moral questions I would never have to face.

When I was around forty, I attended a series of lectures about Carl Jung. I found him to be a proper guide for me on the inner journeys I was to begin during middle age. He was another for whom the last answer was often the next question. He had a boundless imagination and wrote unabashedly about whatever caught his attention. I began to read him with enthusiasm, and I identified with his spiritual struggles because of his upbringing as the son of a Lutheran minister.

The Jungians also liked to sit in a circle, but in chairs. And I could get an honest cup of coffee. The nature of a Jungian group is such that one confronts the material under discussion and never confronts what is said by another member. I found that format much safer. The insights from listening to what others found in a story or piece of music was a tonic to my imagination. Yet that wasn't quite it, either. I had not yet tumbled to my secret: I would find much of my best spiritual growth in words: at first, those of others and later, as my skills improved, in some of my own.

As I have mentioned elsewhere, it was my failure to

write a passable novel that led me by a circuitous route to poetry. Here was the unconscious bubbling forth in metaphors and symbols. Richard Hugo was my first poetic guide because he made room in his life for me and entered mine as well.

My sensibilities are not all that poetic, although I wish at times they were. When I first wrote for the *King County Medical Society Bulletin,* a monthly publication for which I have been editor for a long time, my colleagues commented upon how poetic my writing was. The poets who read the same articles never said that. Only the doctors. I don't think they knew how else to characterize my work and meant it as a compliment. It may also have to do with a popular notion that poets sail a few degrees off true north.

I learned from poets that "making" from within oneself was what was important. The inner life became my concern and I began to make what some call soul. I became an explorer of the interior life, usually dressed wrong for the current expedition. I excelled at missing the obvious and being asleep at the critical moments. My maps were out of date, and my intellect remembered all the wrong things. Gradually I learned how to travel in those lands. Whenever I find an answer it turns out to be the next question for me, also.

III

If I have one credential for writing about medicine it is that medicine is my life's work. I am not a professor or medical scholar nor anyone of particular importance in the over-all scheme of things. I care for patients and am involved in everything that entails. I'm neither better nor worse than most others I know who do this work. But I probably think more about certain aspects of our work, and I write about my thoughts. This is an arrogant thing to do, but I do it.

Nietzche said that we must have illusions in order to live. One illusion that haunts many religious people is that illness is a punishment. An example is the claim that AIDS is God's punishment for homosexuality. The corollary of that illusion is that failure to get well demonstrates a lack of faith. It ranks close to the illusion that all one needs is will power and one can do anything. The invalid insists he will walk one day. He searches for a cure, not for healing as he is.

Some of my most difficult patients are those who believe that their variety of the Christian faith entitles them to miraculous healing. The religious of this kind can leave it all in God's hands. In a way the atheist does the same thing. He, too, says "Goddammit" when he hits his thumb with a hammer. Either position relieves one of personal responsibility and puts the physician in opposition to either the Divine or the power of human will.

One variation on this theme that has troubled me for a long time is so-called "faith healing." There is the television evangelist who shouts into the ear of the supposed arthritic for the demons to come out. These demons must be hard of hearing. I think of this as a magic show, based on deception concocted in private and performed in public. There is an amazing lack of humility in those accomplishing these "miracles." Those who are healed disappear, never to be seen again. Like most entertainment, once it is over the next show begins.

Yet we cannot attribute cures of disease and injury only to the applied science of medicine. Some patients recover while we physicians are bewildered by their progress. A vicious cancer disappears. An apparently hopeless coma resolves into conscious awareness and intellect. This can be explained only partially by our human capacity for error. Mysterious recoveries do occur. Whatever means, medical, religious or otherwise, that were employed during those dark days are usually given credit. These are times when I am happy to have been wrong.

Most discouraging for me is when I have misjudged the seriousness of a patient's condition and things have gone from bad to worse. Again, there is often no explanation. Those who would take credit for finding the effective means in the first case often attribute the worsening to something they are not responsible for: divine will, unkind fate or nature's capriciousness in human matters. In either case the results are unexplainable.

There is no doubt in my mind that we are spiritual beings, and that ignoring our spiritual selves is crippling. But in my experience, the chances for recovery from illnesses and injuries do not depend upon the presence or absence of religious beliefs. Atheists do as well as born-againers. Agnostics have the same chances as Episcopalians.

I have witnessed the most inspired prayer meetings at the bedside of a terminally ill patient end in futility. And I have seen destitute alcoholics survive bout after bout of infection, liver failure and malnutrition, only to weave their way back to the only life they know and resume drinking. The idea of a fatalistic existence where God calls us whenever he chooses and there is nothing we can do about it does not appeal to me, nor jibe with my experience. It makes about as much sense as my diving out of an airplane without a parachute and leaving my fate in God's hands. If he wants to save, he will, and if he doesn't, who am I to complain?

Part of the problem is the confusion of physical health with healing. There are scriptural bases for claims of vision restored to the blind, the crippled walking and Lazarus rising from the dead. I am in no position to debate the theology or even the accuracy of these stories. But I do know that within myself there will always be blindness to cure, crippled parts to restore, deadness to bring to life long after it seems possible to do so.

Yet, there must be more to it than that.

There is an ironic humor in the seriousness with which many Christians take themselves. They are so sure they are right. But being serious doesn't necessarily improve a patient's chances.

On a bad day I could walk the halls of any hospital and curse God for the misery that my patients endure. I find it hard to be on duty at Christmas. The illusion of happy families together in health and excitement crumbles when I watch the palsied try to feed themselves, or the embattled cardiac patient fight for breath.

Sometimes things happen for a purpose and at other times they don't. We live in a world composed of a mixture of determinism and randomness.

IV

There is a difference between healing and curing. In the early flush of medical experience, students and young doctors glow with the prospects of curing the ill. This is a lofty goal, one worthy of our mightiest efforts. But it is not accomplished often. The number of diseases that can be cured by drugs or surgery are quite limited, given the overwhelming number of ways things can malfunction in the human body and the fact that in the end everyone dies. In order to make us feel better, oncologists talk about cancer cures in terms of five-year survival. Certain infections are curable. Duodenal ulcers may heal completely. Minor strokes may leave no detectable residua. Some cancers can be excised and do not recur.

As the years have passed, I have learned to settle for less in the way of cures and more in the way of healing. Healing involves our coming to terms with our mortality and our, at best, gradual decline in physical and mental abilities. Sometimes the changes are sudden, unexpected, even catastrophic. Whatever they are is of concern to the doctor. Healing involves a loss of innocence about what our health and lives are or may become. Long-distance runners die too.

Healing helps us find a place in this world for ourselves and for each other. It removes the distinction between the strong and the weak, the helpless and the ruthless. It teaches us that each of us is as important as anyone else. For healing involves giving a part of myself to the patients and accepting a part of them in return. If healing takes place, neither of us is left the same as we were before we met. Healing is the ongoing growth of spirit and humanness. Now and then a cure might be thrown in, but cures can never replace healing.

Philosopher Martin Buber talks about dialogue between people as forming in a new place, what he calls a "narrow ridge." He maintains that what makes us human is our ability to enter into such dialogue with each other. He calls it an

I-Thou relationship. This is the possibility that sets the stage for healing. The mysteries of how it takes place are enough to keep us speculating for the rest of our lives.

Scientific analysis dries up the blood of the new life that doctor and patient are making. It is that way with any process of creation. The writer must suspend judgement and analysis while putting down the words that want to come forth. Otherwise only the contrived will make its way onto the page. While it may be clever, brilliant and well crafted it will have little or no life of its own. It is that making of life, a form of birthing, that creative acts bring forth. That is what happens between doctors and patients when each both offers and receives.

If doctors and patients spend their time analyzing the doctor-patient relationship instead of experiencing it, there will be much to criticize and little that can grow. A sense of warmth and acceptance between them is only the first step. What follows may not be describable. But it can be recognized and loved for what it is. What happens within the I-Thou dialogue can only be known when it occurs. When writing goes well, the writer is surprised by what appears on the page. Refinement of the work can be done later. First there must be work worth refining.

Doctors and patients are often surprised by what comes forth. The offering to each other of whatever it will take to form the narrow ridge upon which we meet is our work. It is the human means of healing the earth and all that passes within and through our lives. At times the giving is one-sided. Doctors may offer themselves to patients who choose to send nothing back. The patient may get nothing back from the doctor. Maybe nothing of substance will happen. Maybe it shouldn't. Maybe this dialogue is only a step in a process that will take years to unfold. But if we don't search out the possibilities, the chances for healing are reduced if not abolished.

Our lives and the world we live in are the way we think and feel for that moment. Developing our inner lives is only part of our work. Living our lives together by opening deeper and more enlightening experiences and images is one of our most human tasks. Without that, destructiveness can never be modified, only overpowered by even more destructiveness.

Our Lord said that in order to save our lives, we must lose them. What we hold onto is what we most need to give up. We are far more than we believe and far less than we advertise. Poverty of spirit can only be treated when we face what it is and rejoice that it is never too late to be healed once more.

I'm Rejoicing, Carl

DURING the Christmas season, walk down a country road on a clear night and take no flashlight. Depend upon the moon. After all, it's been lighting your way much longer and more reliably than Eveready.

The road in front of my house runs north, the direction of shadows from the winter eye of the sun. It is not as late as it seems and I am dressed in my heavy Cowichan Indian sweater, gloves, a black cap and hair that has more gray in it this year. The wind is slight, crystals of frost sparkle on the blacktop and no clouds interfere with my view of the moon. Ahead, the Big Dipper, handle tilted slightly down, points its two outer stars toward the North Star, which is surprisingly small for all the attention it gets. Power may be more a matter of position than size.

The only sound in the night is the crunch of my footsteps on the frost. Outside an old Victorian farmhouse, I stand and watch the yellow glow from the windows and the Christmas lights on the door and on the tree near the fireplace. Smoke rises straight up from the chimney. I'm invisible here in the dark. I see the people inside and realize I've never met them. I'll not embarrass them by asking for their meaning of Christmas if they promise not to ask for mine.

Overhead, a commercial jet migrates toward the airport, reminding me of flying south from Seattle on a 727 late one October afternoon with endless billows of clouds below like unskied snowfields. The white turns to gray as the sun settles on our right, and we will be late into Phoenix.

Suddenly the plane banks to the left and we circle Mount Hood. The pilot announces that the plane's hydraulic system is not functioning properly and we must return to Seattle-Tacoma Airport for repairs. The passengers are restless and make little jokes. The plane flies smoothly and there is no hint of the pilot sweating over the controls, no dramatic music, just the gentle ride. Can this be the day my life ends?

As we break through the clouds we see the runway lined with fire engines. Yesterday, a DC-10 crashed in Mexico City when it landed on the wrong runway. We laugh with relief as the wheels touch down, the pilot reverses thrust and the plane eases to a stop. Dinner and drinks later, our plane repaired, we take off for another try.

I sit in my seat, 16F, by the window. The wing has an aluminum skin that ripples at this velocity. My seat is as comfortable as a chair at home. If I were blindfolded I could not tell whether I am in the air or on the ground, or that gravity waits to pull us to our deaths if the plane does not maintain sufficient airspeed. Gravity is always waiting for engine failure. Even the driest martini cannot change that.

Poet Robert Bly once told me that if someone went to Carl Jung with news of a new job or other success, Jung would be uninterested. But if someone complained about an unkind turn of fate, injury or illness, Jung's eyes would brighten and he would invite them over for a glass of wine and a discussion of the possibilities.

It is later and the night air feels like snow. More clouds move in and the chill breaks through my sweater. I think of my life and all its failures, the chances I wish I had again but never will. I've made it through another year. My eyes catch the massive head of a Scottish Highlander bull who appears out of the shadows and is barely visible in this light. We watch each other and I smile at his shaggy coat so perfect for whatever turn the winter weather might take.

I say to myself, "I'm rejoicing, Carl! In spite of it all, I've made it again." I wave farewell to the bull, and start for home.

If not available at your
local bookstore, this book may
be ordered by sending $15.95
plus one dollar for postage and handling to:

Madrona Publishers
Department X, P. O. Box 22667
Seattle, WA 98122

Prepaid orders only, please
Add one dollar for postage and handling
for the first book and
fifty cents for each additional book.

Masturcharge and Visa cardholders
may order by calling (206) 325-3973.